Holy Trinity +

We hope you enjoy the music in this book. Further copies are available from your local Kevin Mayhew stockist.

In case of difficulty, or to request a catalogue, please contact the publisher direct by writing to:

The Sales Department
KEVIN MAYHEW LTD
Buxhall
Stowmarket
Suffolk IP14 3BW

Phone 01449 737978
Fax 01449 737834
E-mail info@kevinmayhewltd.com

First published in Great Britain in 2002 by Kevin Mayhew Ltd.

© Copyright 2002 Kevin Mayhew Ltd.

ISBN 1 84003 994 9
ISMN M 57024 143 9
Catalogue No: 1450266

0 1 2 3 4 5 6 7 8 9

Cover design by Jonathan Stroulger

Printed and bound in Great Britain

the British worship collection

kevin mayhew

Important Copyright Information

The Publishers wish to express their gratitude to the copyright owners who have granted permission to include their copyright material in this book. Full details are indicated on the respective pages.

The **words** of most of the songs in this publication are covered by a **Church Copyright Licence** which is available from Christian Copyright Licensing International. This allows local church reproduction on overhead projector acetates, in service bulletins, songsheets, audio/visual recording and other formats.

The **music** in this book is covered by the additional **Music Reproduction Licence** which is issued by CCLI in the territories of Europe and Australasia. You may photocopy the music and words of the songs in the book provided:

You hold a current Music Reproduction Licence from CCLI.

The copyright owner of the song you intend to photocopy is included in the Authorised Catalogue List which comes with your Music Reproduction Licence.

The Music Reproduction Licence is **not** currently available in the USA or Canada.

Full details of CCLI can be obtained from their Web site (www.ccli.com) or you can contact them direct at the following offices:

Christian Copyright Licensing (Europe) Ltd
PO Box 1339, Eastbourne, East Sussex, BN21 1AD, UK
Tel: +44 (0)1323 417711; Fax: +44 (0)1323 417722; E-mail: info@ccli.co.uk

CCL Asia-Pacific Pty Ltd (Australia and New Zealand)
PO Box 6644, Baulkham Hills Business Centre, NSW 2153, Australia
Tel: +61 (02) 9894-5386; Toll Free Phone: 1-800-635-474
Fax: +61 (02) 9894-5701; Toll Free Fax: 1-800-244-477
E-mail executive@ccli.co.au

Christian Copyright Licensing Inc
17201 NE Sacramento Street, Portland, Oregon 97230, USA
Tel: +1 (503) 257 2230; Toll Free Phone: 1 (800) 234 2446;
Fax: +1 (503) 257 2244; E-mail executive@ccli.com

Please note, all texts and music in this book are protected by copyright and if you do <u>not</u> possess a licence from CCLI they may <u>not</u> be reproduced in any way for sale or private use without the consent of the copyright owner.

FOREWORD

'I will bless the Lord at all times: his praise shall be continually in my mouth' Psalm 34:1.

Worship is the highest call there is in all the universe. A lifestyle of continual praise is not just a reasonable response to a loving Saviour, but it is the life-blood of every believer.

For many centuries God has been hallowed on these shores and at various times Great Britain has been a loud-hailer of the message of the gospel to the nations of the world. From the Celtic saints back in the mists of time right through to the Protestant Reformation and then to the more recent history of the Welsh and Hebridean revivals, the British Isles have a spiritual heritage that is as vast as it is rich. Songs and creativity always accompany a move of God and in *The British Worship Collection* we have selected 226 of the best British worship songs. Many of the songs were born out of the Charismatic Movement that started in the 1970s; a time when numerous New Churches came into being and when the Holy Spirit was also breathing new life of Pentecost into the established denominations. This was a time when pioneers like Graham Kendrick emerged, breaking new ground in church music, rediscovering old truths to a new tune and laying the foundation for contemporary Praise and Worship as we know it today. The songs in this collection represent a broad mix ranging from the energetic 'outer courts' type, to the intimacy of the 'secret place'.

Our prayer is that this publication will help to ignite fresh passion for Jesus, enrich the wider church and release worship here 'on earth as it is in heaven'.

RICHARD LEWIS
MAY 2002

1 Abba, Father, let me be

Words and Music: Dave Bilbrough arr. Christopher Tambling

© Copyright 1977 Thankyou Music/Adm. by worshiptogether.com songs excl. UK & Europe, adm. by Kingsway Music. (tym@kingsway.co.uk). Used by permission.

2 All around the world

Words and Music: Paul Oakley

3 All hail the Lamb

Words and Music: Dave Bilbrough

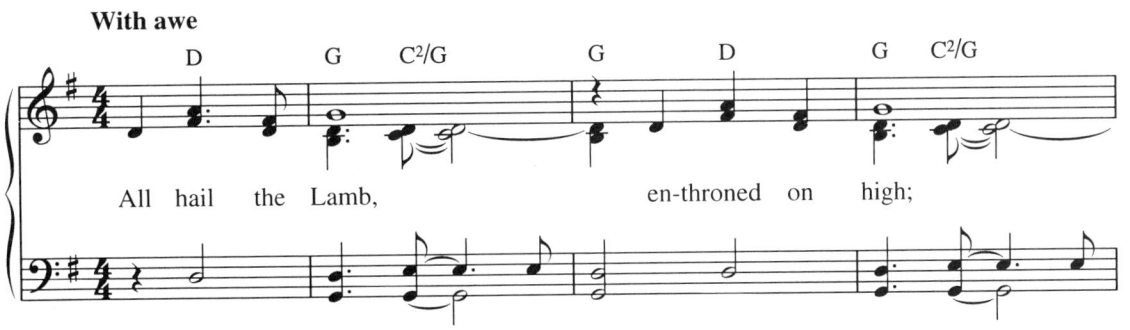

All hail the Lamb, enthroned on high;

his praise shall be our battle cry;

he reigns victorious, forever glorious,

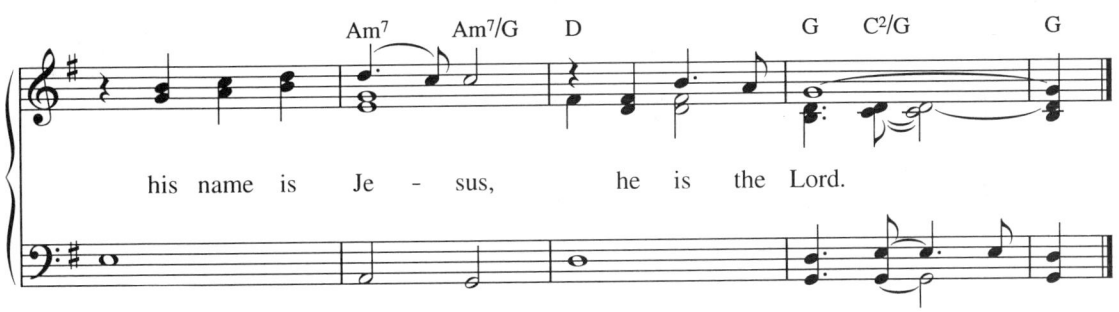

his name is Jesus, he is the Lord.

© Copyright 1988 Thankyou Music/Adm. by worshiptogether.com songs, excl. UK & Europe,
adm. by Kingsway Music. (tym@kingsway.co.uk) Used by permission.

4 All heaven declares

Words and Music: Noel and Tricia Richards

1. All heav'n declares the glory of the risen Lord.
Who can compare with the beauty of the Lord?
For-ever he will be the Lamb upon the throne.
I gladly bow the knee and worship him alone.

2. I will proclaim
the glory of the risen Lord.
Who once was slain
to reconcile us to God.
For ever you will be
the Lamb upon the throne.
I gladly bow the knee
and worship you alone.

© Copyright 1987 Thankyou Music/Adm. by worshiptogether.com songs excl. UK & Europe,
adm. by Kingsway Music. (tym@kingsway.co.uk). Used by permission.

5 All I once held dear
Knowing you

Words and Music: Graham Kendrick

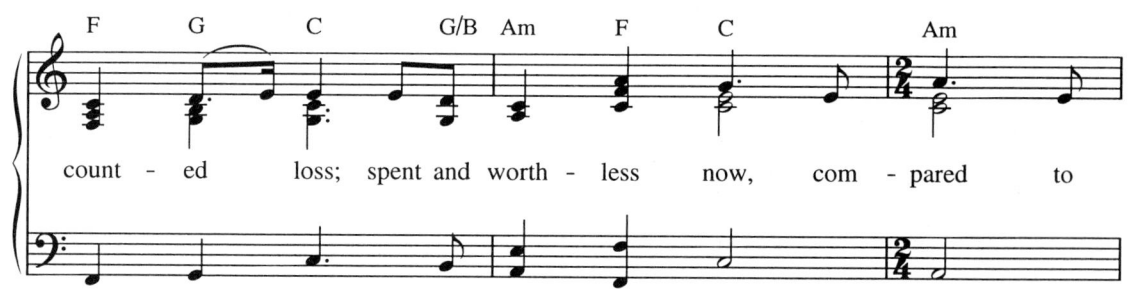

© Copyright 1993 Make Way Music, P.O. Box 263, Croydon, Surrey, CR9 5AP, UK.
International copyright secured. All rights reserved. Used by permission.

2. Now my heart's desire
is to know you more,
to be found in you
and known as yours.
To possess by faith
what I could not earn,
all-surpassing gift
of righteousness.

3. Oh, to know the pow'r
of your risen life,
and to know you in
your sufferings.
To become like you
in your death, my Lord,
so with you to live
and never die.

6 All my days
Beautiful Saviour

Words and Music: Stuart Townend

3. I long to be where the praise is never-ending,
   yearn to dwell where the glory never fades,
   where countless worshippers will share one song,
   and cries of 'worthy' will honour the Lamb!

7 All praise, all honour
All praise

Words and Music: James Wright

© Copyright 2001 Kevin Mayhew Ltd.

8 Amazing love

Words and Music: David Hind

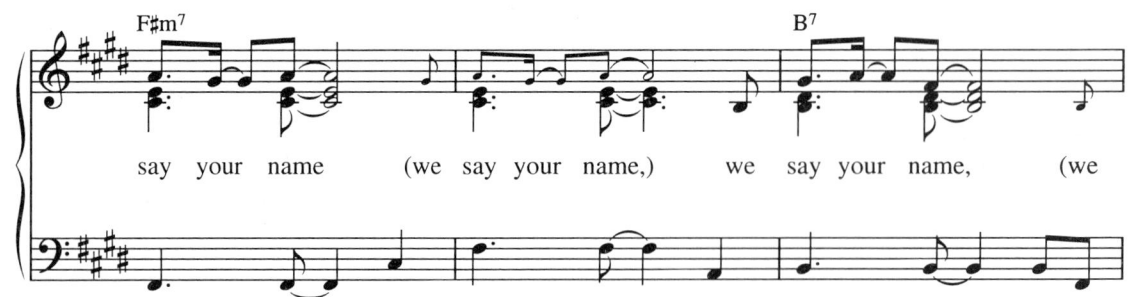

© Copyright 1999 Kevin Mayhew Ltd.

9 Among the gods
You alone are God

Words and Music: Carol Owen

© Copyright 1993 Thankyou Music/Adm. by worshiptogether.com songs excl. UK & Europe, adm. by Kingsway Music. (tym@kingsway.co.uk). Used by permission.

10 An army of ordinary people

Words and Music: Dave Bilbrough

© Copyright 1983 Thankyou Music/Adm. by worshiptogether.com songs excl. UK & Europe, adm. by Kingsway Music. (tym@kingsway.co.uk). Used by permission.

11 As sure as gold is precious
Revival
Words and Music: Robin Mark

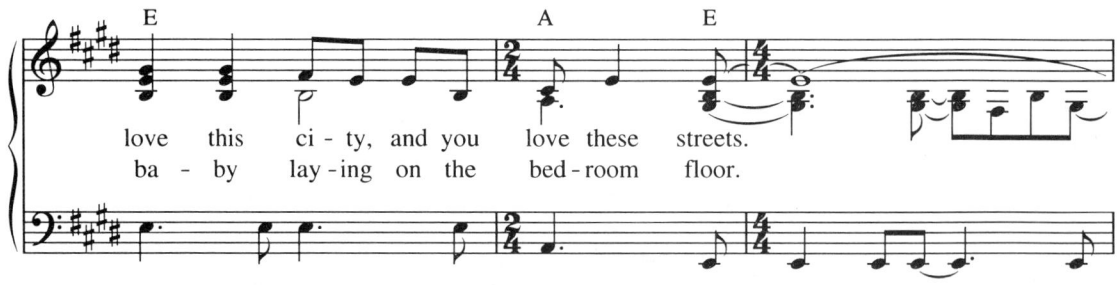

© Copyright 1996 Daybreak Music Ltd. PO Box 2848, Eastbourne, East Sussex, BN20 7XP, UK.
All rights reserved. (info@daybreakmusic.co.uk). International Copyright Secured. Used by permission.

2. From the preacher preaching when the well is dry,
   to the lost soul reaching for a higher high.
   From the young man working through his hopes and fears,
   to the widow walking through the vale of tears.

3. Ev'ry man and woman, ev'ry old and young,
   ev'ry father's daughter, ev'ry mother's son;
   I feel it in my spirit, feel it in my bones,
   you're going to send revival, bring them all back home.

12 As we come to your throne
You are worthy

Words and Music: Andrew Grinnell
arr. Richard Lewis

© Copyright 2001 Kevin Mayhew Ltd.

13 At the foot of the cross

Words and Music: Derek Bond

© Copyright 1992 Sovereign Music UK, P.O. Box 356,
Leighton Buzzard, Bedfordshire, LU7 3WP, UK. Used by permission.

14 At your feet we fall

Words and Music: David Fellingham

© Copyright 1982 Thankyou Music/Adm. by worshiptogether.com songs excl. UK & Europe, adm. by Kingsway Music. (tym@kingsway.co.uk). Used by permission.

2. There we see you stand, mighty risen Lord,
   clothed in garments pure and holy, shining bright.
   Eyes of flashing fire, feet like burnished bronze,
   and the sound of many waters is your voice.

3. Like the shining sun in its noonday strength,
   we now see the glory of your wondrous face.
   Once that face was marred, but now you're glorified,
   and your words like a two-edged sword have mighty pow'r.

15 Awake, awake, O Zion
Our God reigns

Words and Music: Nathan Fellingham

© Copyright 1999 Thankyou Music/Adm. by worshiptogether.com songs excl. UK & Europe, adm. by Kingsway Music. (tym@kingsway.co.uk). Used by permission.

2. How beautiful the feet are
   of those who bring good news,
   for they proclaim the peace that comes from God.
   Rise up you holy nation,
   proclaim the great salvation,
   and say to Zion: 'Your God reigns'.

3. The watchmen lift their voices,
   and raise a shout of joy,
   for he will come again.
   Then all eyes will see the
   salvation of our God,
   for he has redeemed Jerusalem.

16 Be free

Words and Music: Dave Bilbrough

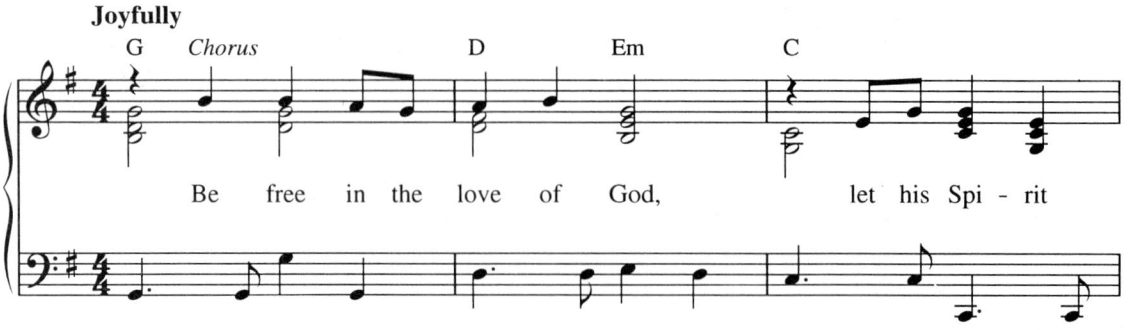

© Copyright 1991 Thankyou Music/Adm. by worshiptogether.com songs excl. UK & Europe, adm. by Kingsway Music. (tym@kingsway.co.uk). Used by permission.

2. God is gracious, he will lead us
through his pow'r at work within us.
Spirit, guide us, and unite us
in the Father's love.

17 Be still, for the presence of the Lord

Words and Music: David J. Evans

1. Be still, for the pre-sence of the Lord, the Ho-ly One is

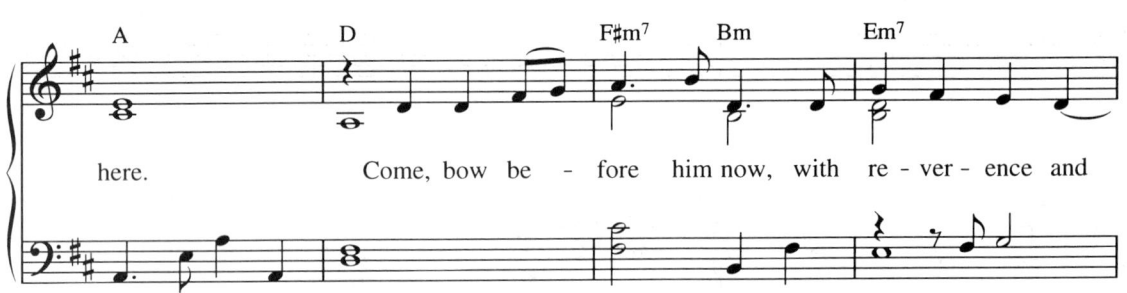
here. Come, bow be-fore him now, with re-ver-ence and

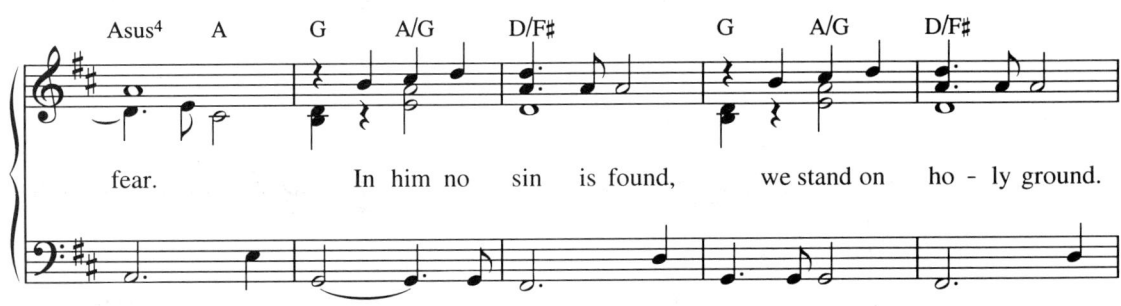
fear. In him no sin is found, we stand on ho-ly ground.

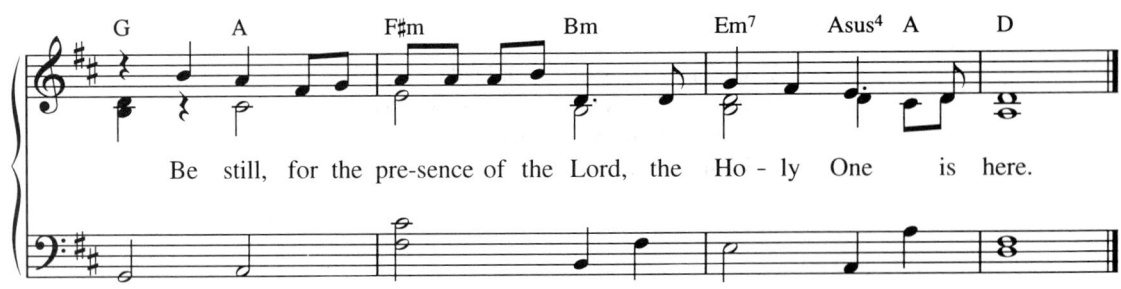
Be still, for the pre-sence of the Lord, the Ho-ly One is here.

© Copyright 1986 Thankyou Music/Adm. by worshiptogether.com songs excl. UK & Europe, adm. by Kingsway Music. (tym@kingsway.co.uk). Used by permission.

2. Be still, for the glory of the Lord is shining all around;
   he burns with holy fire, with splendour he is crowned.
   How awesome is the sight, our radiant King of light!
   Be still, for the glory of the Lord is shining all around.

3. Be still, for the power of the Lord is moving in this place;
   he comes to cleanse and heal, to minister his grace.
   No work too hard for him, in faith receive from him.
   Be still, for the power of the Lord is moving in this place.

18 Blessed are the humble
The beatitudes

Words and Music: Graham Kendrick
arr. Richard Lewis

1. Blessed are the hum-ble in spi-rit,
   blessed are those who hun-ger, who thirst for

jus- tice, for theirs is the King-dom of
       for sure- ly you'll fill them com-

hea- ven. And blessed are the
plet- ely. And those who show

© Copyright 2001 Make Way Music, P.O. Box 263, Croydon, Surrey CR9 5AP, UK.
International copyright secured. All rights reserved. Used by permission.

19 Broken for me

Words and Music: Janet Lunt

© Copyright 1978 Sovereign Music UK, P.O. Box 356,
Leighton Buzzard, Bedfordshire, LU7 3WP, UK. Used by permission.

2. Come to my table and with me dine;
   eat of my bread and drink of my wine.

3. This is my body given for you;
   eat it remembering I died for you.

4. This is my blood I shed for you,
   for your forgiveness, making you new.

20 Broken I stand
Kindle the flame

Words and Music: Jill Sutheran

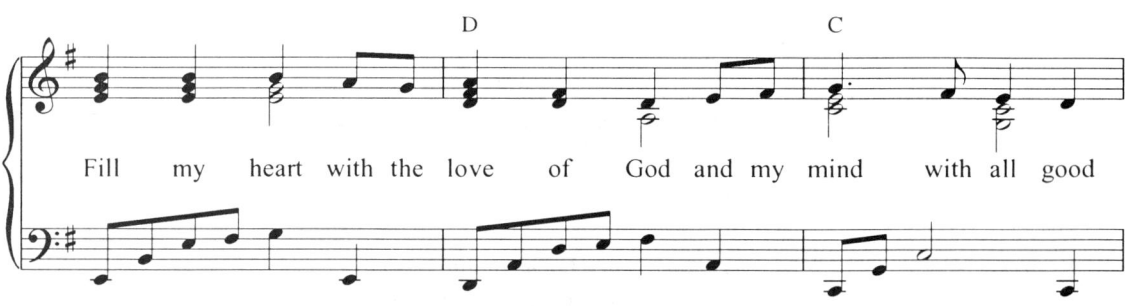

© Copyright 1997 CN Publishing. Administered by CopyCare, P.O. Box 77, Hailsham, BN27 3EF, UK. (music@copycare.com). Used by permission.

21 By your side

Words and Music: Noel and Tricia Richards

© Copyright 1989 Thankyou Music/Adm. by worshiptogether.com songs excl. UK & Europe, adm. by Kingsway Music. (tym@kingsway.co.uk). Used by permission.

22 Can a nation be changed?

Words and Music: Matt Redman

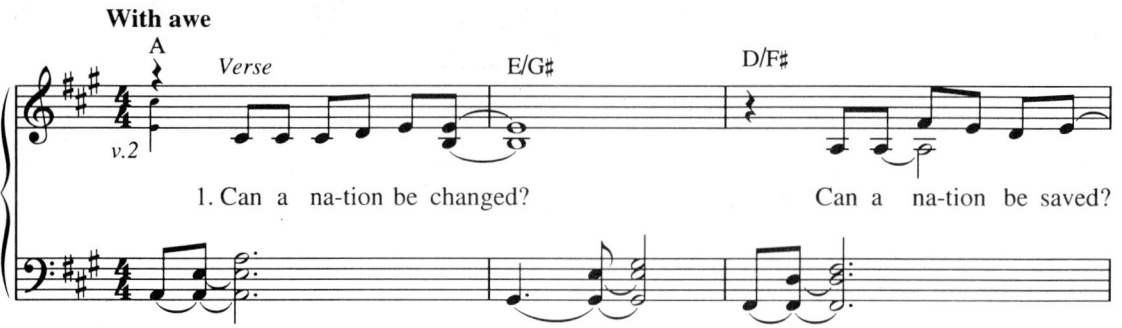

© Copyright 1996 Thankyou Music/Adm. by worshiptogether.com songs excl. UK & Europe, adm. by Kingsway Music. (tym@kingsway.co.uk). Used by permission.

2. Let this nation be changed,
   let this nation be saved,
   let this nation be turned back to you.
   (Repeat)

23 Celebrate in the Lord
Dancing on holy ground

Words and Music: Evan Rogers

© Copyright 2000 Thankyou Music/Adm. by worshiptogether.com songs excl. UK & Europe, adm. by Kingsway Music. (tym@kingsway.co.uk.) Worldwide excluding South Africa. Used by permission.

24 Chosen to go

Words and Music: Susie Hare

© Copyright 2001 Kevin Mayhew Ltd.

25 Come and see

We worship at your feet

Words and Music: Graham Kendrick

© Copyright 1989 Make Way Music, P.O. Box 263, Croydon, Surrey, CR9 5AP, UK.
International copyright secured. All rights reserved. Used by permission.

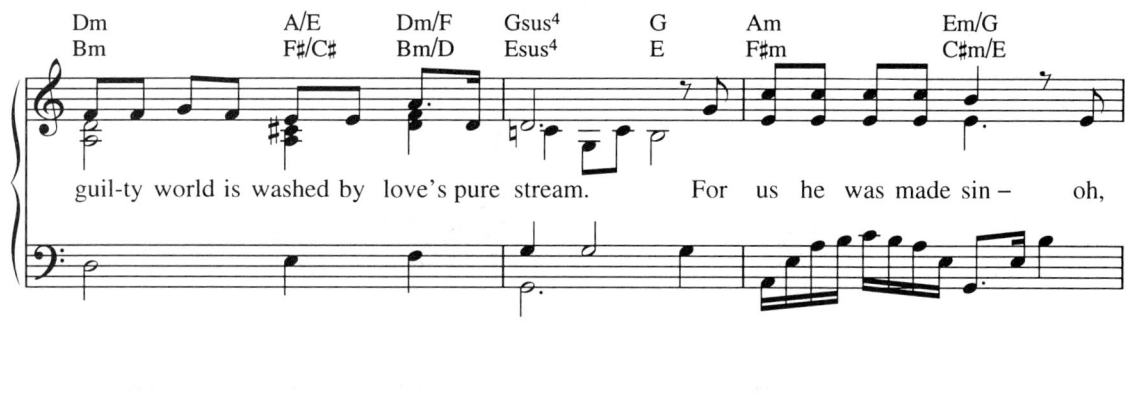

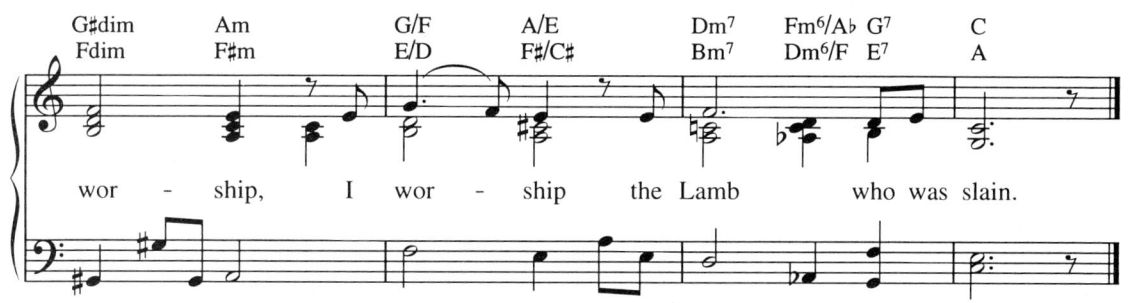

2. Come and weep, come and mourn
   for your sin that pierced him there;
   so much deeper than the wounds of thorn and nail.
   All our pride, all our greed,
   all our fallenness and shame;
   and the Lord has laid the punishment on him.

3. Man of heaven, born to earth
   to restore us to your heaven.
   Here we bow in awe beneath your searching eyes.
   From your tears comes our joy,
   from your death our life shall spring;
   by your resurrection power we shall rise.

26 Come, now is the time to worship

Words and Music: Brian Doerksen

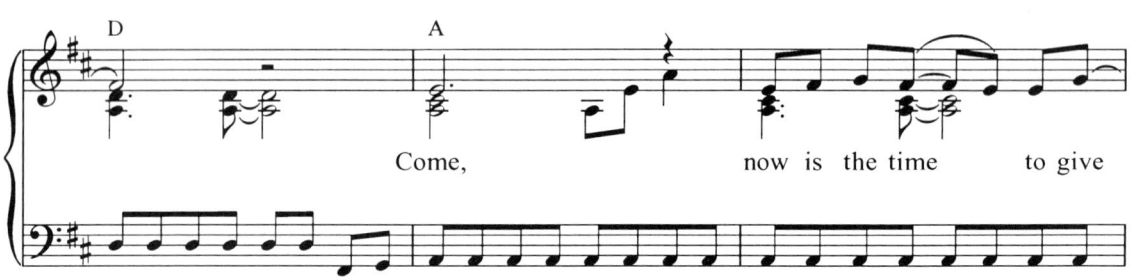

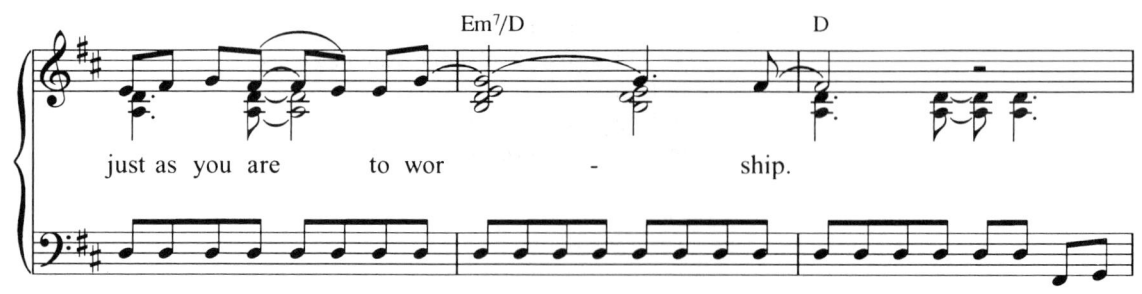

© Copyright 1998 Vineyard Songs (UK/Eire). Administered by CopyCare, P.O. Box 77, Hailsham, East Sussex BN27 3EF. (music@copycare.com). Used by permission.

27 Come on and celebrate
Celebrate

Words and Music: Patricia Morgan and Dave Bankhead

Come on and ce-le-brate his gift of love, we will

ce-le-brate the Son of God who loved us

and gave us life. We'll shout your

praise, O King, you give us joy no-thing else can bring,

© Copyright 1984 Thankyou Music/Adm. by worshiptogether.com songs excl. UK & Europe, adm. by Kingsway Music. (tym@kingsway.co.uk). Used by permission.

28 Creation is awaiting

Words and Music: Chris Bowater and Ian Taylor

© Copyright 1998 Sovereign Lifestyle Music Ltd.,
P.O. Box 356, Leighton Buzzard, Beds, LU7 3WP, UK. Used by permission.

2. The church is awaiting the return of the King.
   The people joined together in his love.
   Redeemed by his blood,
   washed in his word.
   As a bride longs for her bridegroom
   the church looks to God.
   Chorus:
     The King is coming, the King is coming,
     the King is coming to receive his bride. *(x2)*

3. The world is awaiting the return of the King.
   The earth is a footstool for his feet.
   Ev'ry knee will bow down,
   ev'ry tongue confess,
   that Jesus Christ is Lord
   of heaven and earth.
   Chorus:
     The King is coming, the King is coming,
     the King is coming to reign in majesty. *(x2)*

29 Deep within my heart
You are the one

Words and Music: Simon Goodall

© Copyright 1998 Daybreak Music Ltd., P.O. Box 2848, Eastbourne, East Sussex BN20 7XP, UK.
All rights reserved. (info@daybreakmusic.co.uk). International copyright secured. Used by permission.

2. Once we were apart
   then you found me
   and made me your own.
   All this world had to offer
   couldn't match the love you've shown.

30 Did you feel the mountains tremble?

Words and Music: Martin Smith

© Copyright 1994 Curious? Music UK. PO Box 40, Arundel,
West Sussex BN18 0UQ, UK. Used by permission.

31 Faithful God

Words and Music: Chris Bowater

© Copyright 1990 Sovereign Lifestyle Music Ltd, P.O. Box 356, Leighton Buzzard,
Bedfordshire, LU7 3WP, UK. Used by permission.

32 Far and near
Say it loud

Words and Music: Graham Kendrick

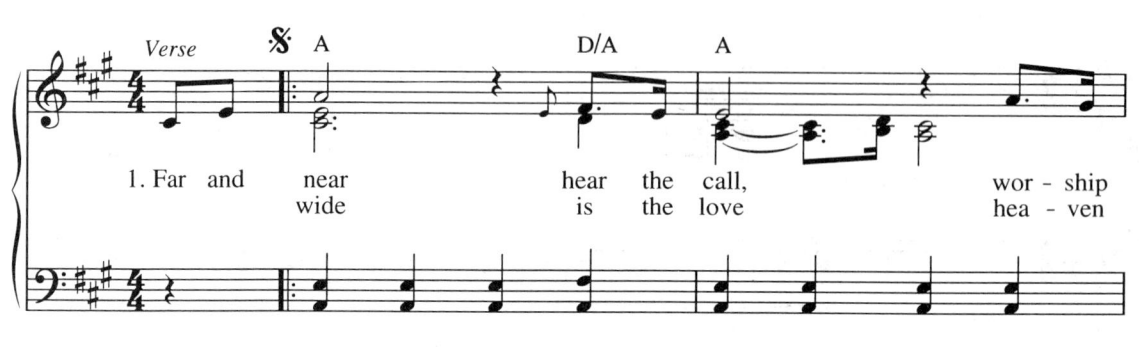
1. Far and near hear the call, worship
   wide is the love heaven

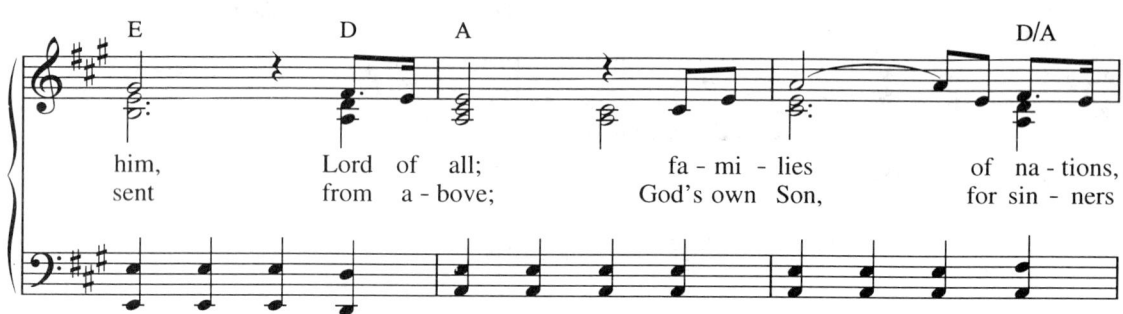
him, Lord of all; fa-mi-lies of na-tions,
sent from a-bove; God's own Son, for sin-ners

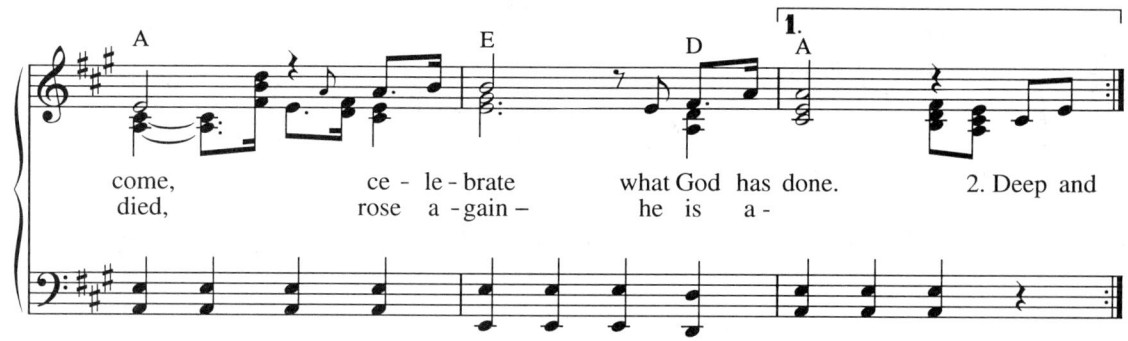
come, ce-le-brate what God has done. 2. Deep and
died, rose a-gain – he is a-

live. Say it loud, say it strong, tell the

© Copyright 1996 Make Way Music, P.O. Box 263, Croydon, Surrey, CR9 5AP, UK.
International copyright secured. All rights reserved. Used by permission.

3. At his name, let praise begin;
oceans roar, nature sing,
for he comes to judge the earth
in righteousness and in his truth.

33 Father God, I wonder
I will sing your praises
Words and Music: Ian Smale

© Copyright 1984 Thankyou Music/Adm. by worshiptogether.com songs excl. UK & Europe, adm. by Kingsway Music. (tym@kingsway.co.uk). Used by permission.

34 Father, to you
What grace

Words and Music: Graham Kendrick
arr. Richard Lewis

Copyright © 2000 Make Way Music, PO Box 263, Croydon, Surrey CR9 5AP, UK.
International copyright secured. All rights reserved. Used by permission.

2. Deep is the joy that fills your courts above,
   while angels wonder at your redeeming love;
   and, as you gaze with joy upon your Son,
   your eyes are on the ones his love has won.

3. No higher call than to be heirs with him,
   so let our passion burn for heavenly things.
   Seated with Christ, for him alone to live,
   our hearts for ever where our treasure is.

35 For riches of salvation
Give thanks

Words: Martin E. Leckebusch
Music: Susie Hare

FROYLE 75 75 777 7

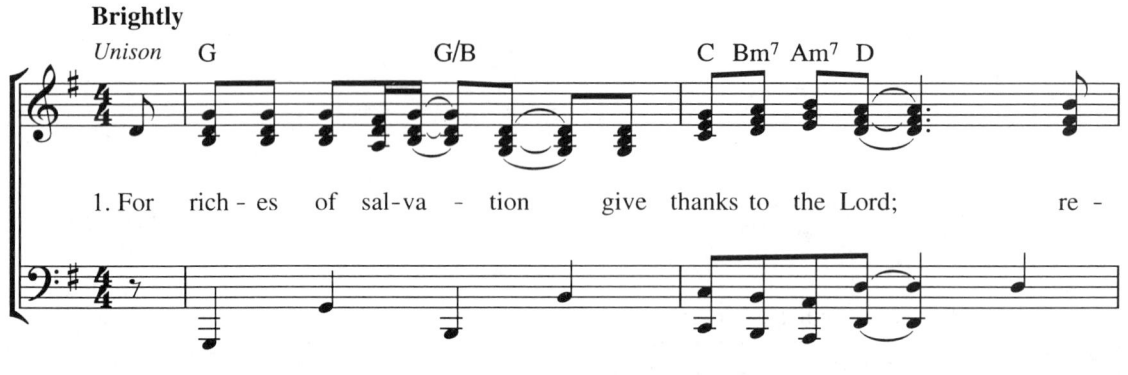

1. For rich-es of sal-va-tion give thanks to the Lord; re-

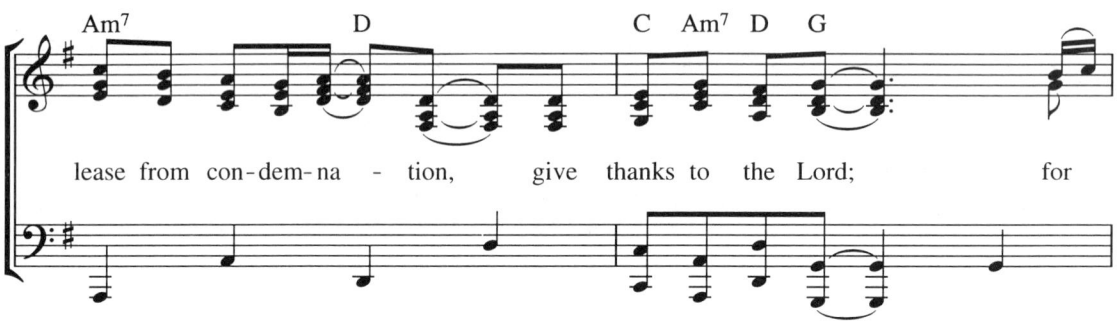

lease from con-dem-na-tion, give thanks to the Lord; for

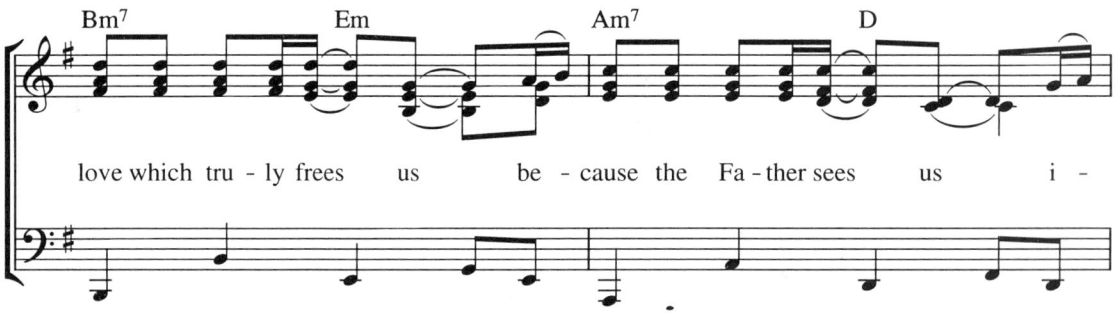

love which tru-ly frees us be-cause the Fa-ther sees us i-

den-ti-fied with Je-sus— give thanks, give thanks to the Lord!

© Copyright 2001 Kevin Mayhew Ltd.

2. For courage and endurance
   give thanks to the Lord;
   the Spirit's reassurance,
   give thanks to the Lord;
   for fatherly correction,
   the call to share perfection,
   the hope of resurrection –
   give thanks, give thanks to the Lord!

3. For life in all its fullness
   give thanks to the Lord;
   for all that leads to wholeness,
   give thanks to the Lord;
   he knows our ev'ry feeling
   and speaks in grace, revealing
   his comfort and his healing –
   give thanks, give thanks to the Lord!

4. For justice with compassion
   give thanks to the Lord,
   and freedom from oppression,
   give thanks to the Lord;
   for holiness unending,
   a kingdom still extending,
   all earthly pow'r transcending –
   give thanks, give thanks to the Lord!

36 For this purpose

Words and Music: Graham Kendrick

© Copyright 1985 Thankyou Music/Adm. by worshiptogether.com songs excl. UK & Europe, adm. by Kingsway Music. (tym@kingsway.co.uk). Used by permission.

2. In the name of Jesus we stand,
   by the power of his blood
   we now claim this ground.
   Satan has no authority here,
   pow'rs of darkness must flee,
   for Christ has the victory.

37 For you have been our hope
Sovereign Lord

Words and Music: Ian Roberts

© Copyright 1999 Kevin Mayhew Ltd.

38 Friend of sinners

Words and Music: Matt Redman

© Copyright 1994 Thankyou Music/Adm. by worshiptogether.com songs excl. UK & Europe, adm. by Kingsway Music. (tym@kingsway.co.uk). Used by permission.

39 From heaven you came
The Servant King
Words and Music: Graham Kendrick

© Copyright 1983 Thankyou Music/Adm. by worshiptogether.com songs excl. UK & Europe, adm. by Kingsway Music. (tym@kingsway.co.uk). Used by permission.

2. There in the garden of tears,
   my heavy load he chose to bear;
   his heart with sorrow was torn.
   'Yet not my will but yours,' he said.

3. Come see his hands and his feet,
   the scars that speak of sacrifice,
   hands that flung stars into space,
   to cruel nails surrendered.

4. So let us learn how to serve,
   and in our lives enthrone him;
   each other's needs to prefer,
   for it is Christ we're serving.

40 From the heights of glory
What a gift
Words and Music: Susie Hare

2. From a humble stable, to a world of shame,
   the friend of sinners, who calls my name
   brought the love of heaven to the hearts of men
   and it gave lives hope again.

3. From a life, so perfect, to a cruel cross,
   the world's redemption, the Father's loss;
   and the nails were driven and the blood flowed free
   in the hands outstretched for me.

4. From the grave he's risen, ever glorified,
   to take his place at his Father's side;
   and the greatest glory will be ours to own
   when he comes to take us home.

What a hope, what a hope we are given,
sacrifice of the Father for us.
What a song to proclaim: 'He is risen!
King of kings, Lord of lords, Jesus!
King of kings, Lord of lords, Jesus!'

41 From the squalor of a borrowed stable
Immanuel

Words and Music: Stuart Townend

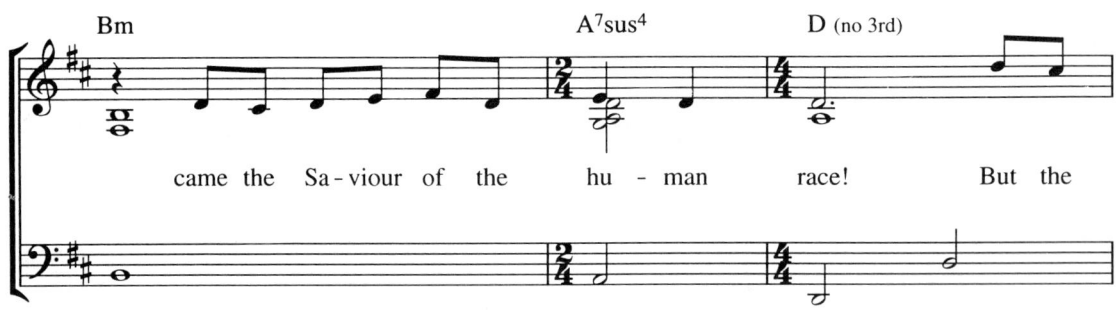

© Copyright 1999 Thankyou Music/Adm. by worshiptogether.com songs excl. UK & Europe, adm. by Kingsway Music. (tym@kingsway.co.uk). Used by permission.

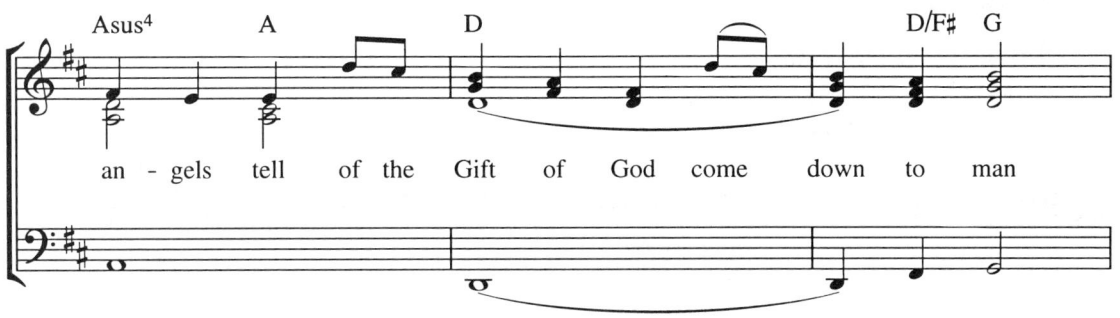

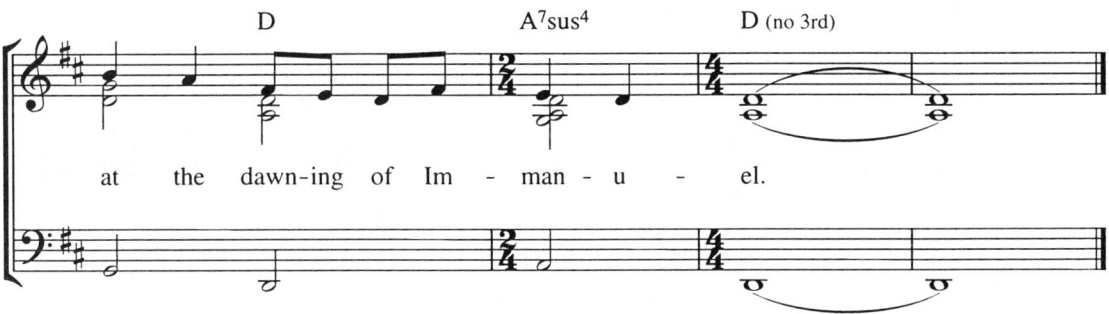

2. King of heaven now the friend of sinners,
   humble servant in the Father's hands,
   filled with power and the Holy Spirit,
   filled with mercy for the broken man.
   Yes, he walked my road and he felt my pain,
   joys and sorrows that I know so well;
   yet his righteous steps give me hope again –
   I will follow my Immanuel!

3. Through the kisses of a friend's betrayal,
   he was lifted on a cruel cross;
   he was punished for a world's transgressions,
   he was suffering to save the lost.
   He fights for breath, he fights for me,
   loosing sinners from the claims of hell;
   and with a shout our souls are free –
   death defeated by Immanuel!

4. Now he's standing in the place of honour,
   crowned with glory on the highest throne,
   interceding for his own belovèd
   till his Father calls to bring them home!
   Then the skies will part as the trumpet sounds
   hope of heaven or the fear of hell;
   but the Bride will run to her Lover's arms,
   giving glory to Immanuel!

2. Giver of hope, rock of salvation,
   tower of refuge, yet there in my pain.
   Now I'm secure, loved for eternity,
   showered with blessings
   and lavished with grace.

43 God is good

Words and Music: Graham Kendrick

© Copyright 1985 Thankyou Music/Adm. by worshiptogether.com songs excl. UK & Europe, adm. by Kingsway Music. (tym@kingsway.co.uk) Used by permission.

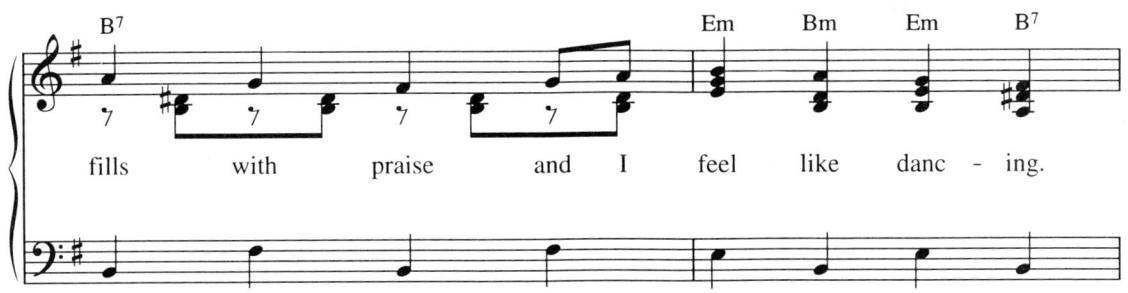

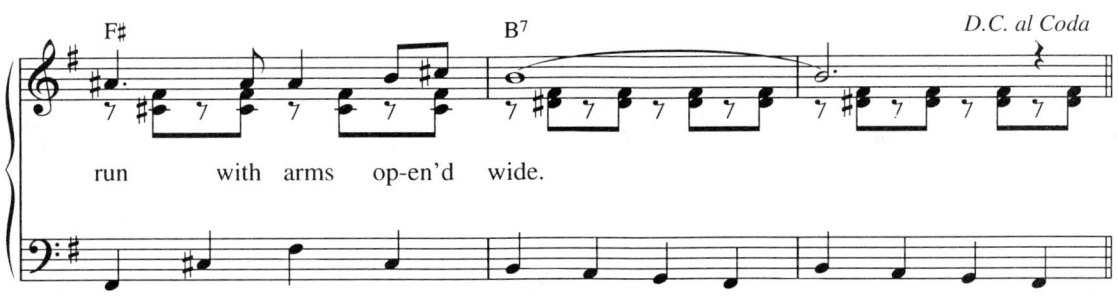

44 God of glory, we exalt your name

Words and Music: David Fellingham

© Copyright 1982 Thankyou Music/Adm. by worshiptogether.com songs excl. UK & Europe, adm. by Kingsway Music. (tym@kingsway.co.uk). Used by permission.

45 God of grace
I stand complete in you

Words and Music: Chris Bowater

© Copyright 1990 Sovereign Lifestyle Music Ltd, P.O. Box 356, Leighton Buzzard, Bedfordshire, LU7 3WP. Used by permission.

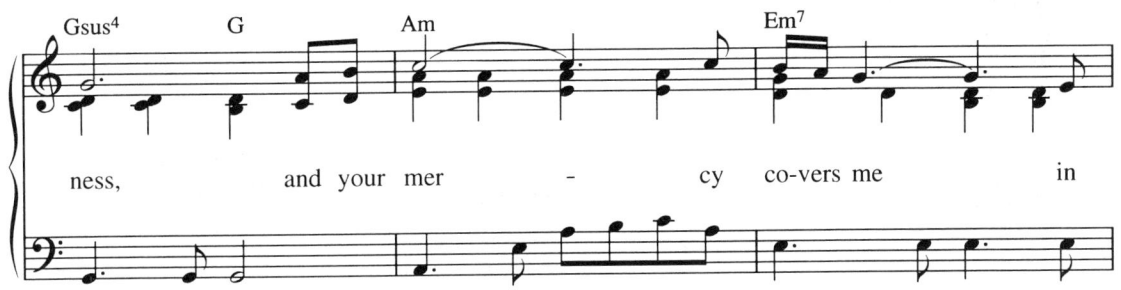

46 Greater grace

Words and Music: Chris Bowater

© Copyright 1999 Sovereign Lifestyle Music Ltd., Leighton Buzzard, Bedfordshire, LU7 3WP, UK. Used by permission.

47 Great is the darkness
Come, Lord Jesus
Words and Music: Noel Richards and Gerald Coates

© Copyright 1992 Thankyou Music/Adm. by worshiptogether.com songs excl. UK & Europe,
adm. by Kingsway Music. (tym@kingsway.co.uk). Used by permission.

2. May now your church rise with power and love,
   this glorious gospel proclaim.
   In ev'ry nation salvation will come
   to those who believe in your name.
   Help us bring light to this world
   that we might speed your return.

3. Great celebrations on that final day
   when out of the heavens you come.
   Darkness will vanish, all sorrow will end,
   and rulers will bow at your throne.
   Our great commission complete,
   then face to face we shall meet.

48 Great is your name
Only you deserve the glory

Words and Music: Jarrod Cooper

© Copyright 1994 Deep Blue Publishing/Sovereign Music UK. PO Box 356,
Leighton Buzzard, LU7 3WP, UK. Used by permission.

2. Faithful and true in all you do, O Lord.
   Saviour and King, my ev'rything, my all.
   There is none like you,
   who loves the way you do, Jehovah.

49 Have you heard the good news

Words and Music: Stuart Garrard

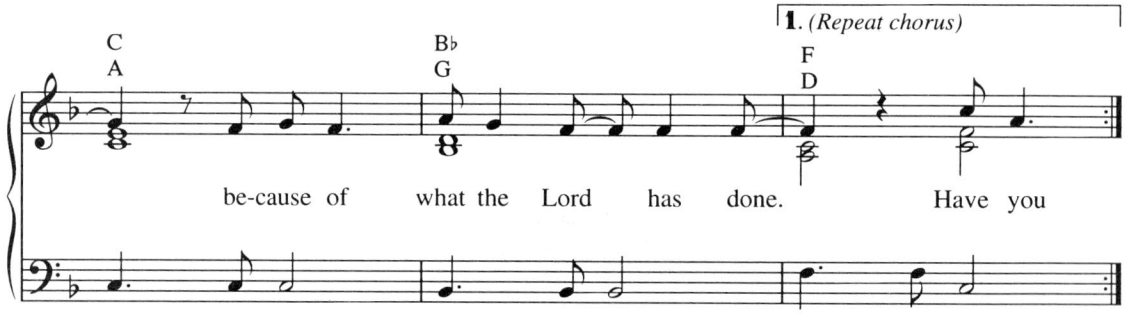

© Copyright 1995 Curious? Music UK. PO Box 40, Arundel, West Sussex BN18 0UQ.
Used by permission.

50 He has risen

Words and Music: Gerald Coates, Noel Richards and Tricia Richards

© Copyright 1993 Thankyou Music/Adm. by worshiptogether.com songs excl. UK & Europe, adm. by Kingsway Music. (tym@kingsway.co.uk). Used by permission.

2. In the grave God did not leave him,
   for his body to decay;
   raised to life, the great awakening,
   Satan's pow'r he overcame.

3. If there were no resurrection,
   we ourselves could not be raised;
   but the Son of God is living,
   so our hope is not in vain.

4. When the Lord rides out of heaven,
   mighty angels at his side,
   they will sound the final trumpet,
   from the grave we shall arise.

5. He has given life immortal,
   we shall see him face to face;
   through eternity we'll praise him,
   Christ the champion of our faith.

51 He is holy, holy, holy
Holy, holy, holy

Words and Music: Ken Riley

With a driving rhythm

He is ho-ly, ho-ly, ho-ly, my Lord is

ho-ly, ho-ly, ho-ly, Je-sus. Give

glo-ry, glo-ry, glo-ry to the Son,

3rd time to Bridge
Last time to Coda

glo-ry, glo-ry, glo-ry to Je-sus!

© Copyright 1999 Thankyou Music/Adm. by worshiptogether.com songs excl. UK & Europe, adm. by Kingsway Music. (tym@kingsway.co.uk). Used by permission.

52 Here I am

Words and Music: Chris Bowater

© Copyright 1982 Sovereign Lifestyle Music,
P.O. Box 356, Leighton Buzzard, Beds., LU7 3WP, UK. Used by permission.

2. The time is right in the nation
   for works of power and authority;
   God's looking for a people who are willing
   to be counted in his glorious victory.

3. As salt are we ready to savour,
   in darkness are we ready to be light?
   God's seeking out very special people
   to manifest his truth and his might.

53 Here I am
I will always love your name

Words and Music: Paul Oakley

Rhythmically

1. Here I am, and I have come to thank you, Lord, for all you've done: thank you, Lord; you paid the price at Cal-va-ry, you shed your blood, you set me free: thank you, Lord; no

© Copyright 1997 Thankyou Music/Adm. by worshiptogether.com songs excl. UK & Europe, adm. by Kingsway Music. (tym@kingsway.co.uk). Used by permission.

2. You took my sin, you took my shame,
   you drank my cup, you bore my pain:
   thank you, Lord;
   you broke the curse, you broke the chains,
   in victory from death you rose again:
   thank you, Lord;
   and not by works, but by your grace
   you clothe me now in your righteousness.

3. You bid me come, you make me whole,
   you give me peace, you restore my soul:
   thank you, Lord;
   you fill me up, and when I'm full
   you give me more till I overflow:
   thank you, Lord;
   you're making me to be like you,
   to do the works of the Father, too.

54 Here is the risen Son

Words and Music: Michael Sandeman

© Copyright 1997 Thankyou Music/Adm. by worshiptogether.com songs excl. UK & Europe, adm. by Kingsway Music. (tym@kingsway.co.uk). Used by permission.

55 He rides on the wings of the wind
Consuming fire

Words and Music: Richard Lewis

© Copyright 2001 Kevin Mayhew Ltd.

2. His hair is as white as the snow, his eyes are a flame of fire;
holy is he, holy is he.
His feet are like glowing bronze, his voice like the many waters;
holy is he, holy is he.

56 He's given me a garment of praise

Words and Music: David Hadden

© Copyright 1994 Restoration Music Ltd. Administered by Sovereign Music UK,
P.O. Box 356, Leighton Buzzard, Bedfordshire, LU7 3WP, UK. Used by permission.

57 Holy, holy, so holy

Words and Music: Richard Lewis

© Copyright 2001 Kevin Mayhew Ltd.

58 Holy Spirit, we wait on you

Words and Music: Andrew Rayner
arr. Richard Lewis

© Copyright 2001 Kevin Mayhew Ltd.

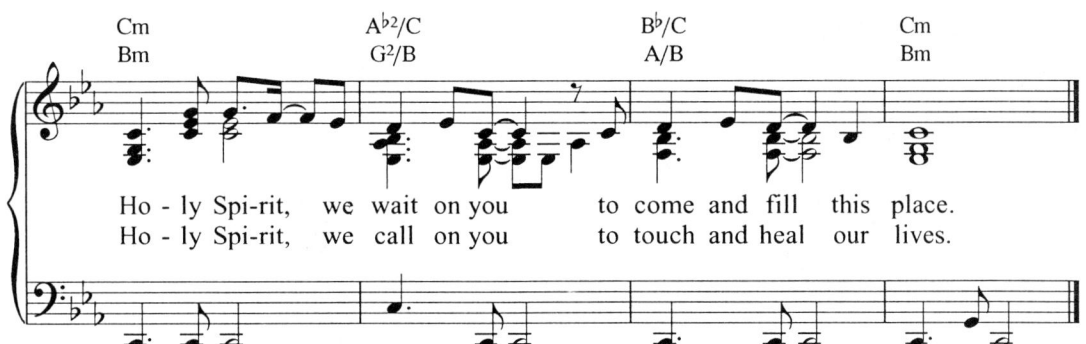

59 Holy Spirit, we welcome you

Words and Music: Chris Bowater

© Copyright 1986 Sovereign Lifestyle Music Ltd, P.O. Box 356,
Leighton Buzzard, Bedfordshire, LU7 3WP, UK. Used by permission.

2. Holy Spirit, we welcome you.
   Holy Spirit, we welcome you.
   Let the breeze of your presence blow,
   that your children here might truly know
   how to move in the Spirit's flow.
   Holy Spirit, Holy Spirit,
   Holy Spirit, we welcome you.

3. Holy Spirit, we welcome you.
   Holy Spirit, we welcome you.
   Please accomplish in me today
   some new work of loving grace, I pray;
   unreservedly have your way.
   Holy Spirit, Holy Spirit,
   Holy Spirit, we welcome you.

60 How can I be free from sin?
Lead me to the cross

Words and Music: Graham Kendrick and Steve Thompson

1. How can I be free from sin? Lead me to the cross of Jesus, from the guilt, the pow'r, the pain, lead me to the cross of Jesus.

There's no o-ther way, no price that I could pay,

© Copyright 1991 Make Way Music, P.O. Box 263, Croydon, Surrey CR9 5AP, UK.
International copyright secured. All rights reserved. Used by permission.

2. How can I know peace within?
   Lead me to the cross of Jesus,
   sing a song of joy again,
   lead me to the cross of Jesus.

   Flowing from above,
   all-forgiving love,
   from the Father's heart to me.
   What a gift of grace,
   his own righteousness,
   clothing me in purity.

3. How can I live day by day?
   Lead me to the cross of Jesus,
   following his narrow way,
   lead me to the cross of Jesus.

61 How deep the Father's love for us

Words and Music: Stuart Townend

2. Behold the man upon a cross,
   my sin upon his shoulders;
   ashamed, I hear my mocking voice
   call out among the scoffers.
   It was my sin that held him there
   until it was accomplished;
   his dying breath has brought me life –
   I know that it is finished.

3. I will not boast in anything,
   no gifts, no pow'r, no wisdom;
   but I will boast in Jesus Christ,
   his death and resurrection.
   Why should I gain from his reward?
   I cannot give an answer,
   but this I know with all my heart,
   his wounds have paid my ransom.

62 How lovely is your dwelling-place
Better is one day
Words and Music: Matt Redman

© Copyright 1995 Thankyou Music/Adm. by worshiptogether.com songs excl. UK & Europe,
adm. by Kingsway Music. (tym@kingsway.co.uk). Used by permission.

63 Hungry, I come to you
Falling on my knees

Words and Music: Kathryn Scott
arr. Chris Mitchell

(♩ = 86)

1. Hun-gry, I come to you, for I know you sat-is-fy.

I am emp-ty, but I know your love

does not run dry. So I wait for you;

so I wait for you. I'm fal-

© Copyright 1999 Vineyard Songs (UK/Eire). Administered by CopyCare, P.O. Box 77, Hailsham, East Sussex BN27 3EF. (music@copycare.com). Used by permission.

2. Broken, I run to you,
   for your arms are open wide.
   I am weary, but I know
   your touch restores my life.
   So I wait for you;
   so I wait for you.

64 I am a new creation

Words and Music: Dave Bilbrough

65 I am learning

Words and Music: Susie Hare

2. I am learning, Lord, that in your plan for me,
   I must learn acceptance of the things that are to be;
   I am learning, Lord, whatever life may ask,
   you will give me strength enough
   to arm me for my task.

3. I am learning, Lord, that in your plan for me,
   all that I will ever do should for your glory be;
   I am learning, Lord, to put my trust in you;
   even when the way is hard,
   your grace will take me through.

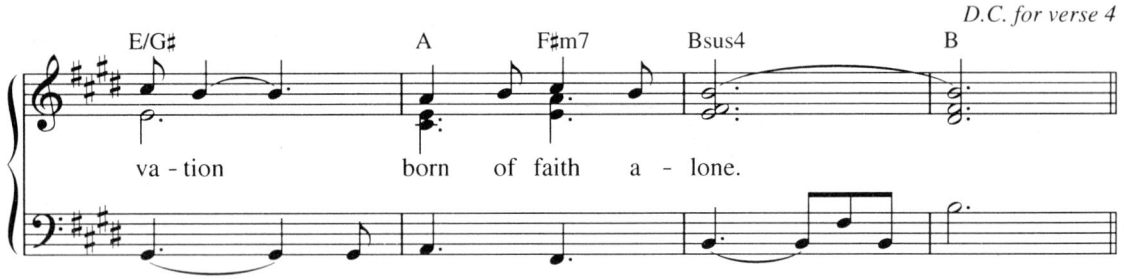
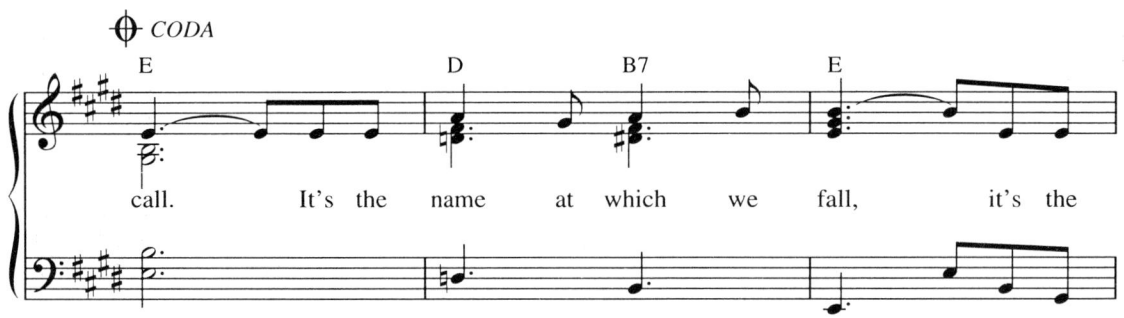
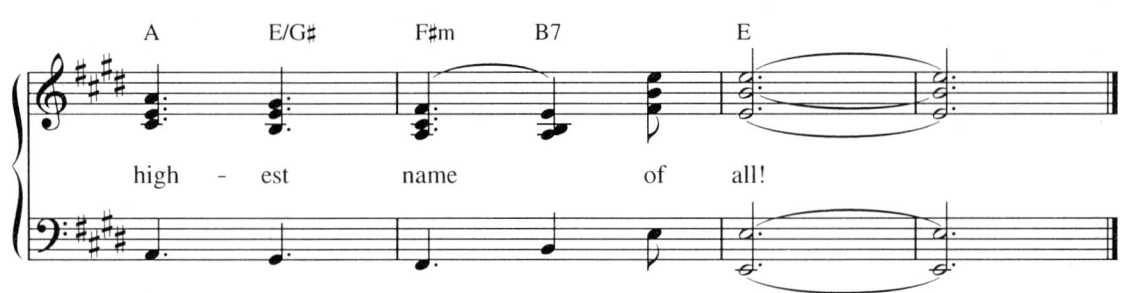

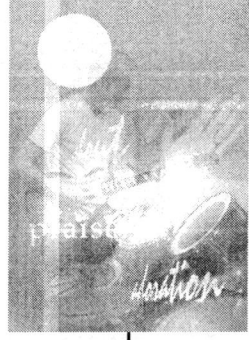

67 I believe in the gospel
We believe

Words and Music: David Hind

© Copyright 2000 Kevin Mayhew Ltd.

2. We believe there is mercy;
   we believe there is hope.
   We believe in forgiveness,
   that God's grace still shines forth.
   So we pray, Father, come now,
   release your fire, your Spirit in our land.
   We believe in Jesus Christ,
   the Son of God, he is alive.

3. We believe in the Church,
   it's the body of Christ on the earth.
   We believe there is one way,
   there's one faith, one baptism, one Lord.
   So we pray, Father, come now,
   release your fire, your Spirit in our land.
   We believe in Jesus Christ,
   the Son of God, he is alive.

Last Chorus:
So here he comes; this is his city
let the King now come in.
Open our eyes, he is alive;
see the King now come in.

68 I could sing unending songs
The happy song
Words and Music: Martin Smith

© Copyright 1994 Curious? Music UK. PO Box 40, Arundel,
West Sussex BN18 0UQ, UK. Used by permission.

69 I delight

Words and Music: Chris Bowater

© Copyright 1981 Sovereign Lifestyle Music, P.O. Box 356,
Leighton Buzzard, Beds., LU7 3WP, UK. Used by permission.

70 I have heard so many songs
The Father's song

Words and Music: Matt Redman

© 2000 Thankyou Music/Adm. by worshiptogether.com songs excl. UK & Europe, adm. by Kingsway Music. (tym@kingsway.co.uk). Used by permission.

71 I lift my eyes to the quiet hills

Words: Timothy Dudley-Smith
from Psalm 121

Music: Michael Baughen
Elisabeth Crocker

DAVOS 458 457

1. I lift my eyes to the quiet hills in the press of a busy day; as green hills stand in a dusty land so God is my strength and stay.

2. I lift my eyes
   to the quiet hills
   to a calm that is mine to share;
   secure and still
   in the Father's will
   and kept by the Father's care.

3. I lift my eyes
   to the quiet hills
   with a prayer as I turn to sleep;
   by day, by night,
   through the dark and light
   my Shepherd will guard his sheep.

4. I lift my eyes
   to the quiet hills
   and my heart to the Father's throne;
   in all my ways
   to the end of days
   the Lord will preserve his own.

Text © Copyright Timothy Dudley-Smith in Europe (including UK and Ireland) and in all territories not controlled by Hope Publishing Company. Music © Copyright Michael Baughen/Jubilate Hymns, 4 Thorne Park Road, Chelston, Torquay TQ2 6RX. Used by permission.

72 I'm accepted, I'm forgiven

Words and Music: Rob Hayward

© Copyright 1985 Thankyou Music/Adm. by worshiptogether.com songs excl. UK & Europe, adm. by Kingsway Music. (tym@kingsway.co.uk). Used by permission.

73 I'm forever in your love

Words and Music: Doug Horley
arr. Dave Bankhead

© Copyright 1999 Thankyou Music/Adm. by worshiptogether.com songs excl. UK & Europe,
adm. by Kingsway Music. (tym@kingsway.co.uk). Used by permission.

74 In Christ alone

Words: Stuart Townend
Music: Keith Getty

© Copyright 2001 Thankyou Music/Adm. by worshiptogether.com songs excl. UK & Europe, adm. by Kingsway Music. (tym@kingsway.co.uk). Used by permission.

2. In Christ alone! – who took on flesh,
   fullness of God in helpless babe!
   This gift of love and righteousness,
   scorned by the ones he came to save:
   till on that cross as Jesus died,
   the wrath of God was satisfied
   for ev'ry sin on him was laid:
   here in the death of Christ I live.

3. There in the ground his body lay,
   Light of the world by darkness slain:
   then bursting forth in glorious day
   up from the grave he rose again!
   And as he stands in victory
   sin's curse has lost its grip on me,
   for I am his and he is mine –
   bought with the precious blood of Christ.

4. No guilt in life, no fear in death,
   this is the pow'r of Christ in me;
   from life's first cry to final breath,
   Jesus commands my destiny.
   No pow'r of hell, no scheme of man,
   can ever pluck me from his hand;
   till he returns or calls me home,
   here in the pow'r of Christ I'll stand!

75 Is it true today
History maker
Words and Music: Martin Smith

© Copyright 1996 Curious? Music UK. PO Box 40, Arundel, West Sussex BN18 0UQ, UK.
Used by permission.

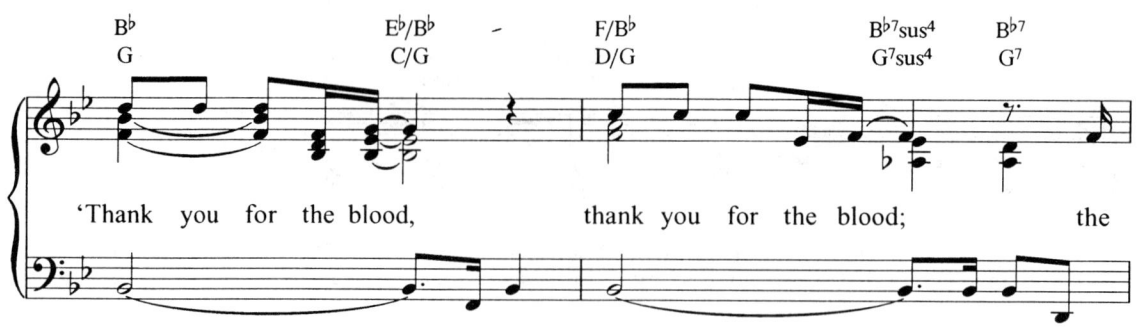
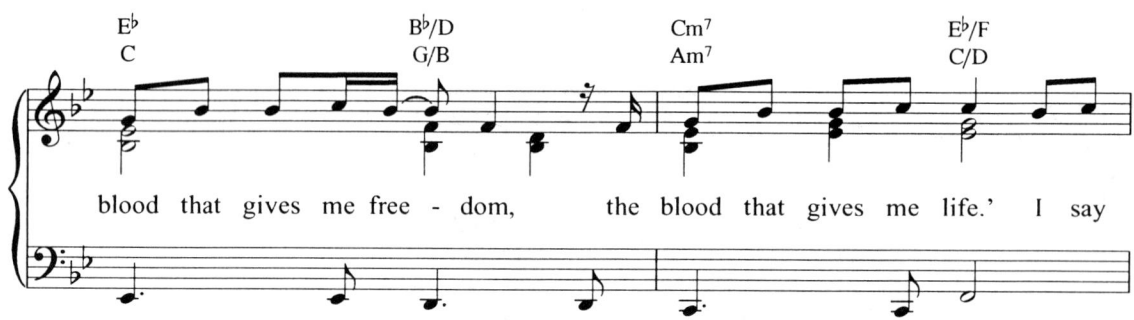
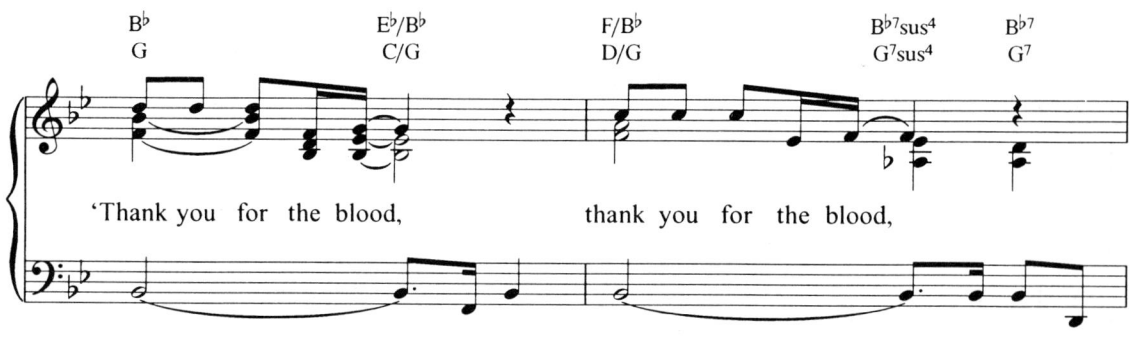

77 It's rising up

Words and Music: Matt Redman and Martin Smith

3. And we have heard the lion's roar,
   that speaks of heaven's love and pow'r.
   Is this the time, is this the call
   that ushers in your kingdom rule?
   O let the cry to nations ring,
   that all may come and all may sing:
       'Jesus is alive!' (Ev'ry heart sing:)
       'Jesus is alive!' (With one voice sing:)
       'Jesus is alive!' (All the earth sing:)
       'Jesus is alive!'

78 I've thrown it all away
Take the world but give me Jesus

Words and Music: Matt Redman

79 I want to be out of my depth in your love

Words and Music: Doug Horley and Noel Richards

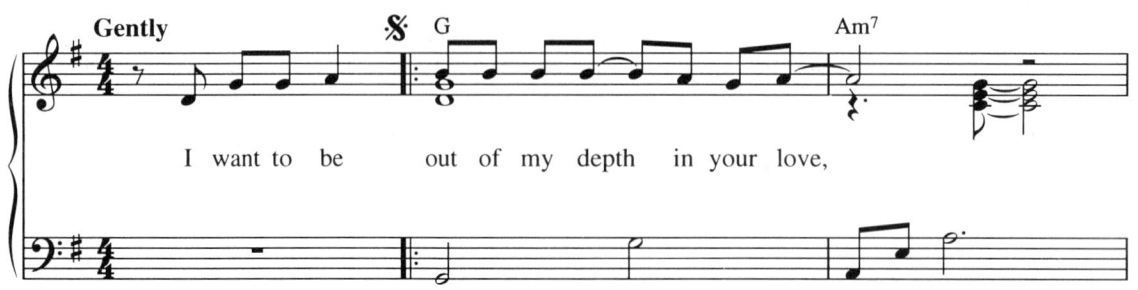

I want to be out of my depth in your love,

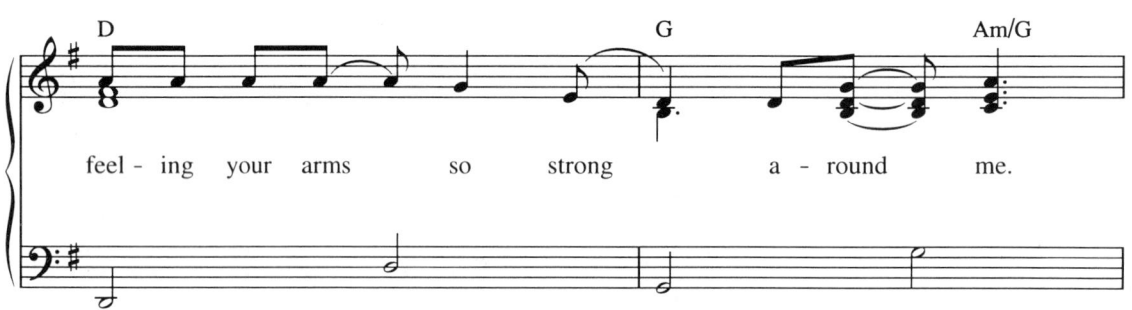

feel-ing your arms so strong a-round me.

Out of my depth in your love, out of my depth in you.

1. I want to be
2. Learn-ing to let
   Things I have held

© Copyright 1995 Thankyou Music/Adm. by worshiptogether.com songs excl. UK & Europe, adm. by Kingsway Music. (tym@kingsway.co.uk). Used by permission.

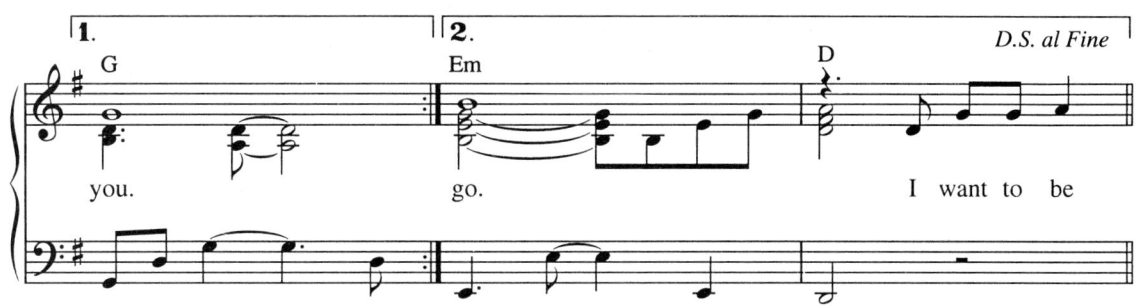

80 I will awaken the dawn

Words and Music: Richard Lewis

© Copyright 2001 Kevin Mayhew Ltd.

81 I will dance, I will sing
Undignified
Words and Music: Matt Redman

© Copyright 1995 Thankyou Music/Adm. by worshiptogether.com songs excl. UK & Europe,
adm. by Kingsway Music. (tym@kingsway.co.uk). Used by permission.

82 I will love you for the cross
For the cross

Words and Music: Matt and Beth Redman

© Copyright 1998 Thankyou Music/Adm. by worshiptogether.com songs excl. UK & Europe, adm. by Kingsway Music. (tym@kingsway.co.uk). Used by permission.

83 I will offer up my life
This thankful heart
Words and Music: Matt Redman

© Copyright 1994 Thankyou Music/Adm. by worshiptogether.com songs excl. UK & Europe, adm. by Kingsway Music. (tym@kingsway.co.uk). Used by permission.

2. You deserve my ev'ry breath
   for you've paid the great cost;
   giving up your life to death,
   even death on a cross.
   You took all my shame away,
   there defeated my sin,
   opened up the gates of heav'n,
   and have beckoned me in.

84 I will sing of your love

Words and Music: Dave Wellington

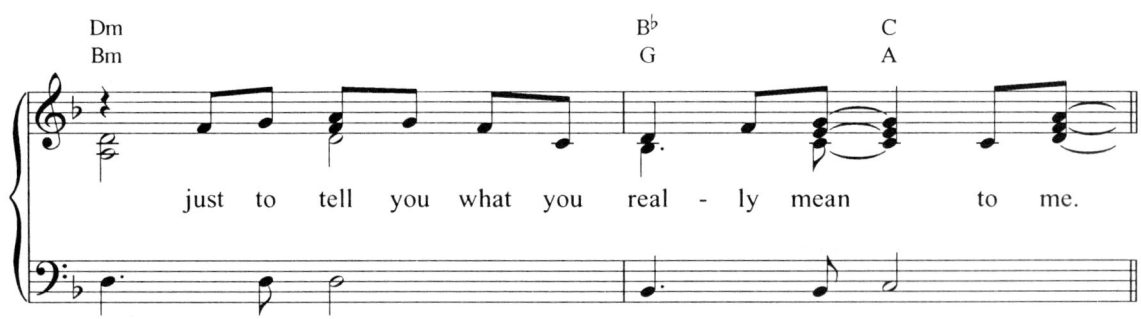

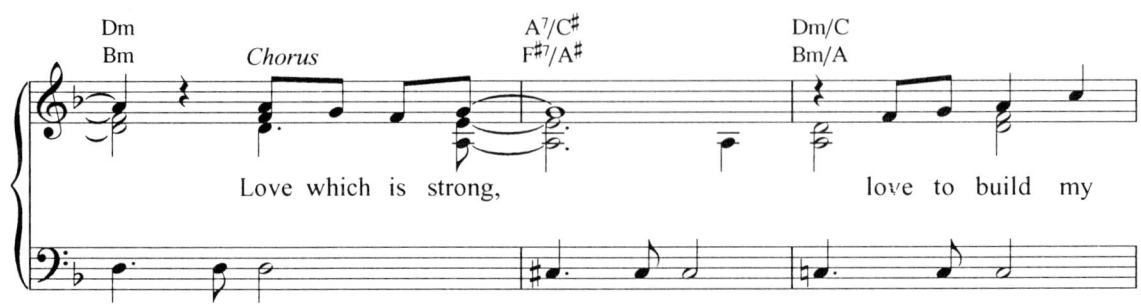

© Copyright 1998 Run Deep Music. Administered by CopyCare, P.O. Box 77,
Hailsham, East Sussex BN27 3EF, UK. (music@copycare.com). Used by permission.

2. I will sing of your love,
   love with passion,
   love with ever-living flame.
   I will sing of your love,
   from the rooftops
   I will sing and shout your name.

3. I will sing of your love,
   love with power,
   love with grace to make me change.
   I will sing of your love,
   with such mercy
   can I ever be the same?

85 I will testify

Words and Music: Richard Lewis

© Copyright 2001 Kevin Mayhew Ltd.

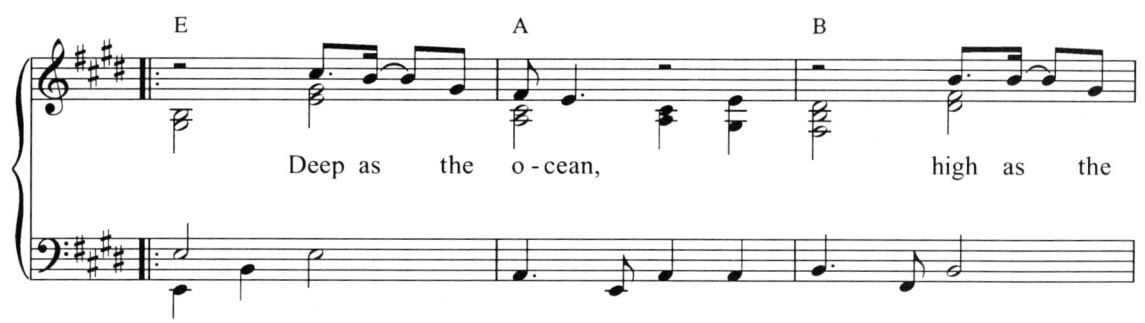

86 Jesus, all for Jesus

Words and Music: Jennifer Atkinson and Robin Mark

© Copyright 1991 Word's Spirit of Praise Music. Administered by CopyCare,
P.O. Box 77, Hailsham, East Sussex BN27 3EF UK. (music@copycare.com). Used by permission.

87 Jesus, at your name
You are the Christ

Words and Music: Chris Bowater

Jesus, at your name we bow the knee.
Jesus, at your name we bow the knee.
Jesus, at your name we bow the knee, and acknowledge you as Lord.
You are the Christ, you are the Lord.
Through your Spirit in our lives we know who you are.

© Copyright 1982 Sovereign Lifestyle Music Ltd, P.O. Box 356,
Leighton Buzzard, Bedfordshire, LU7 3WP, UK. Used by permission.

88 Jesus, be the centre
Be the centre

Words and Music: Michael Frye
arr. Chris Mitchell

© Copyright 1999 Vineyard Songs (UK/Eire). Administered by CopyCare,
P.O. Box 77, Hailsham, East Sussex BN27 3EF. (music@copycare.com). Used by permission.

3. Jesus, be my vision,
   be my path, be my guide,
   Jesus.

89 Jesus Christ
Once again
Words and Music: Matt Redman

© Copyright 1995 Thankyou Music/Adm. by worshiptogether.com songs excl. UK & Europe, adm. by Kingsway Music. (tym@kingsway.co.uk). Used by permission.

2. Now you are exalted to the highest place,
   King of the heavens, where one day I'll bow.
   But for now I marvel at this saving grace,
   and I'm full of praise once again,
   I'm full of praise once again.

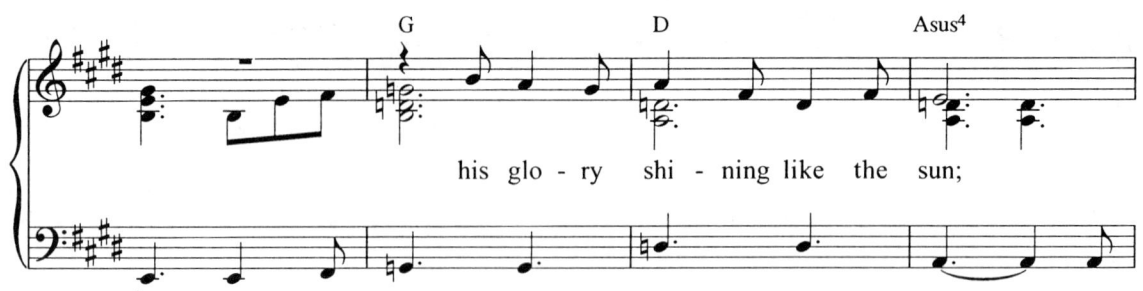

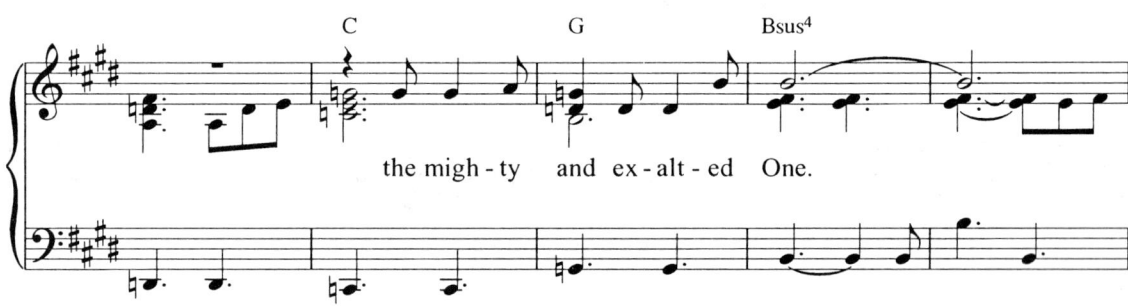

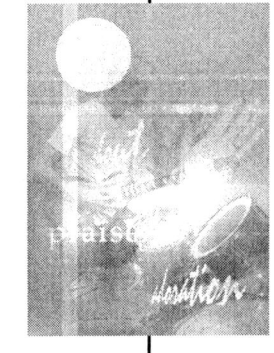

91 Jesus is the name we honour
Jesus is our God
Words and Music: Philip Lawson Johnston

© Copyright 1991 Thankyou Music/Adm. by worshiptogether.com songs excl. UK & Europe, adm. by Kingsway Music. (tym@kingsway.co.uk). Used by permission.

2. Jesus is the name we worship;
   Jesus is the name we trust.
   He is the King above all other kings,
   let all creation stand and sing
   that Jesus is our God.

3. Jesus is the Father's splendour;
   Jesus is the Father's joy.
   He will return to reign in majesty,
   and ev'ry eye at last will see
   that Jesus is our God.

92 Jesus, King of the ages
Prophet, Priest and King

Words and Music: David Lyle Morris and Faith Forster

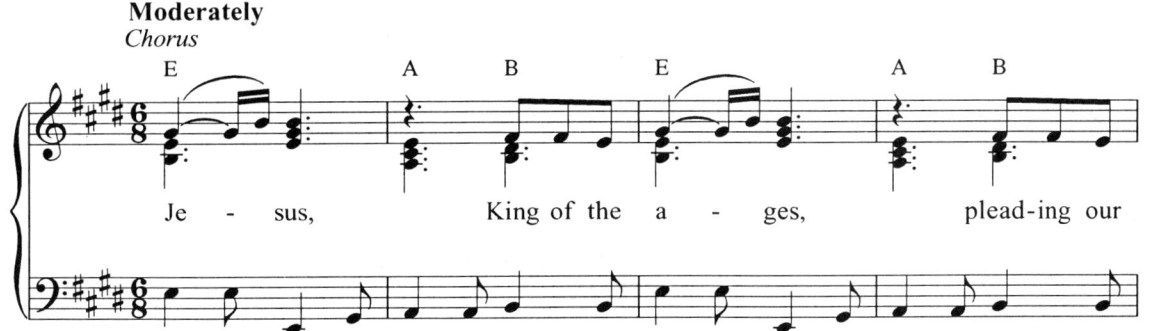
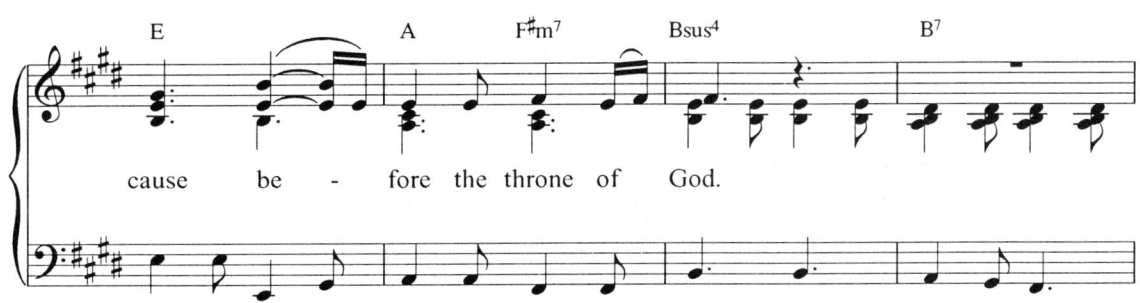

© Copyright 2000 Thankyou Music/Adm. by worshiptogether.com songs excl. UK & Europe,
adm. by Kingsway Music. (tym@kingsway.co.uk). Used by permission.

93 Jesus, lover of my soul
It's all about you
Words and Music: Paul Oakley

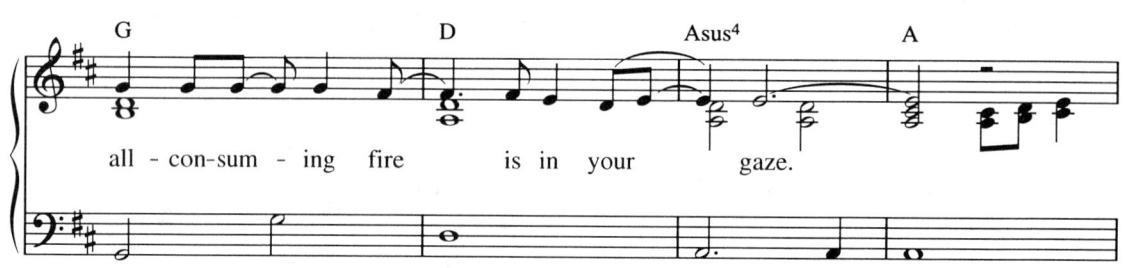

© Copyright 1995 Thankyou Music/Adm. by worshiptogether.com songs excl. UK & Europe, adm. by Kingsway Music. (tym@kingsway.co.uk). Used by permission.

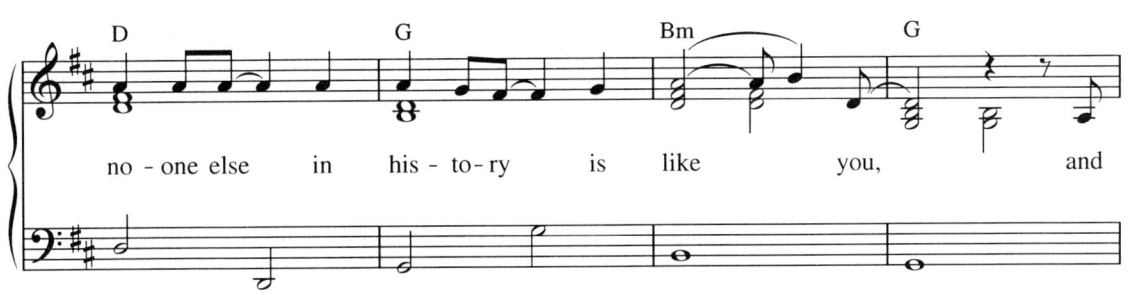

94 Jesus put this song into our hearts

Words and Music: Graham Kendrick

2. Jesus taught us how to live in harmony,
   Jesus taught us how to live in harmony,
   diff'rent faces, diff'rent races, he made us one,
   Jesus taught us how to live in harmony.

3. Jesus taught us how to be a family,
   Jesus taught us how to be a family,
   loving one another with the love that he gives,
   Jesus taught us how to be a family.

4. Jesus turned our sorrow into dancing,
   Jesus turned our sorrow into dancing,
   changed our tears of sadness into rivers of joy,
   Jesus turned our sorrow into a dance.

© Copyright 1986 Thankyou Music/Adm. by worshiptogether.com songs excl. UK & Europe,
adm. by Kingsway Music. (tym@kingsway.co.uk). Used by permission.

95 Jesus shall take the highest honour

Words and Music: Chris Bowater

© Copyright 1988 Sovereign Lifestyle Music Ltd, P.O. Box 356,
Leighton Buzzard, Bedfordshire, LU7 3WP, UK. Used by permission.

96 Jesus, take me as I am

Words and Music: Dave Bryant

Je-sus, take me as I am, I can

come no o-ther way. Take me deep-er in-to you,

make my flesh life die a-way.

Make me like a pre-cious stone, crys-tal

© Copyright 1978 Thankyou Music/Adm. by worshiptogether.com songs excl. UK & Europe,
adm. by Kingsway Music. (tym@kingsway.co.uk). Used by permission.

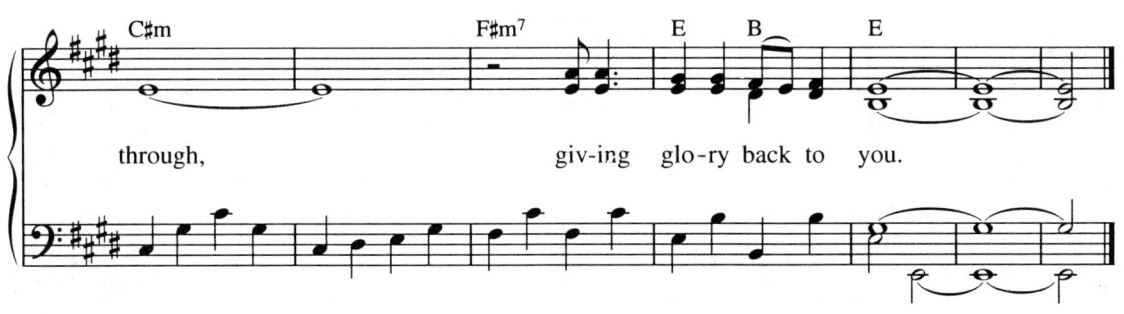

97 Jesus, the Holy One

Words and Music: Susie Hare

© Copyright 2001 Kevin Mayhew Ltd.

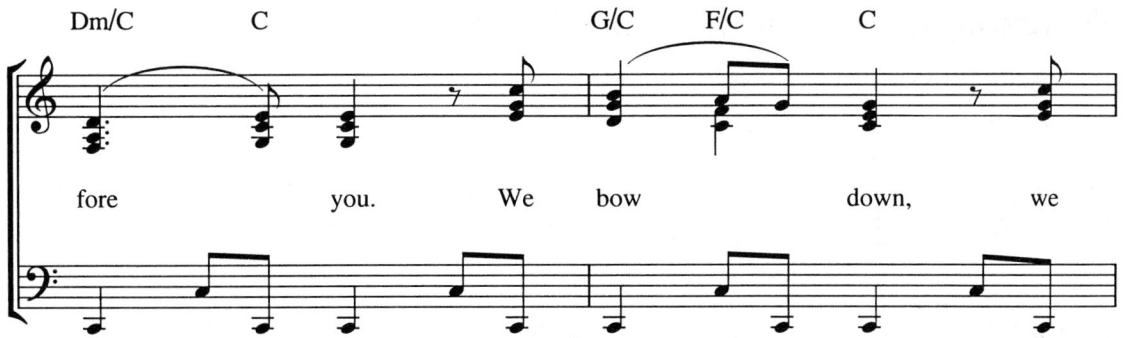
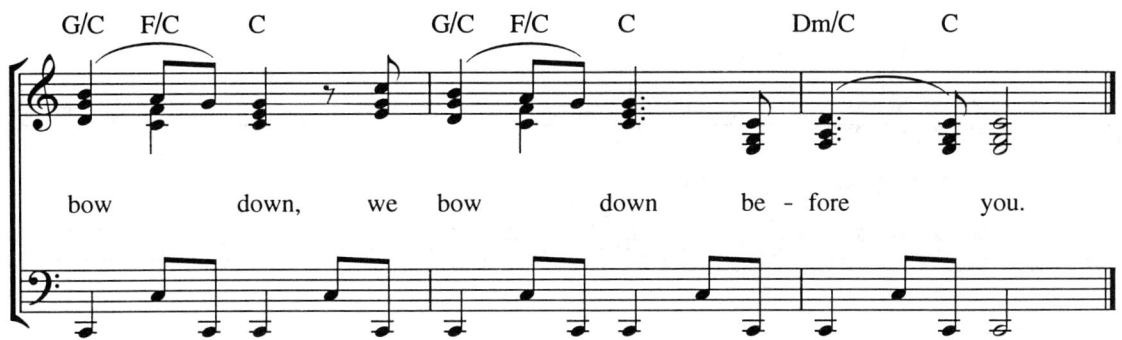

2. Jesus, the Holy Lamb,
   the sacrifice of God for man.
   Jesus, the Holy Lamb,
   we bow before you now.

3. Jesus, the holy name
   that takes our sin, that bears our shame.
   Jesus, the holy name,
   we bow before you now.

2. His Spirit in us releases us from fear,
   the way to him is open, with boldness we draw near.
   And in his presence our problems disappear;
   our hearts responding to his love.

99 Jesus, we enthrone you

Words and Music: Paul Kyle

Je - sus, we en - throne you,

we pro - claim you our King,

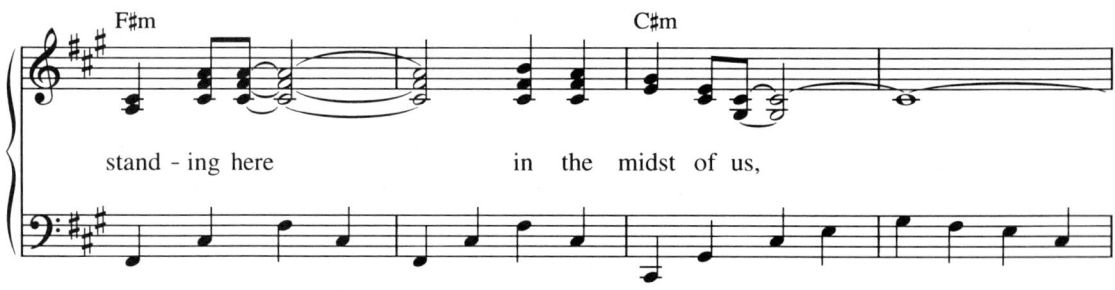

stand - ing here in the midst of us,

we raise you up with our praise.

© Copyright 1980 Thankyou Music/Adm. by worshiptogether.com songs excl. UK & Europe, adm. by Kingsway Music. (tym@kingsway.co.uk). Used by permission.

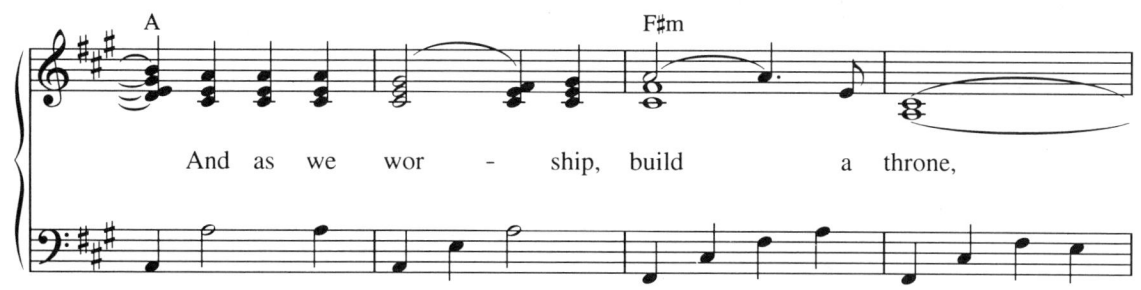
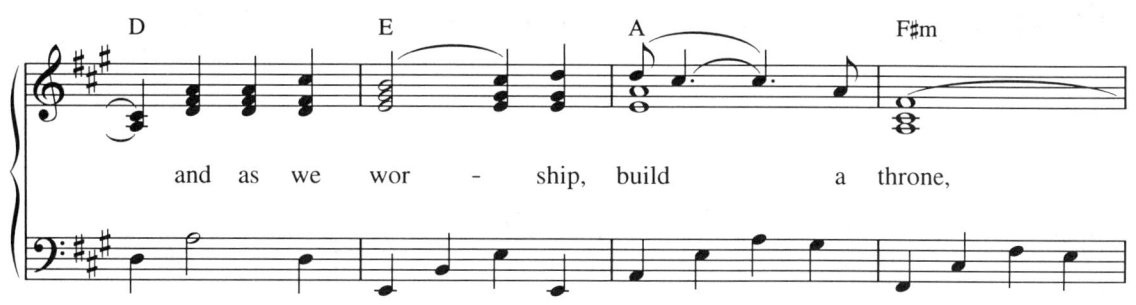
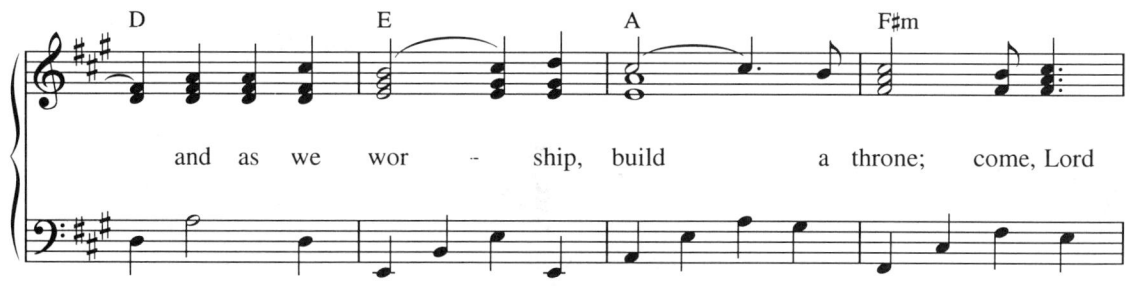

100 Jesus, you alone

Words and Music: Tim Hughes

101 Jesus, you are changing me

Words and Music: Marilyn Baker

© Copyright 1981 Springtide/Word Music UK, a division of Word UK Ltd.
Administered by CopyCare, PO Box 77, Hailsham, East Sussex BN27 3EF, UK. Used by permission.

102 Jesus, you are Lord of heaven
You are so good

Words and Music: Paul Banderet
arr. Richard Lewis

1. Je - sus, you are Lord of hea - ven

yet to earth you glad - ly came.

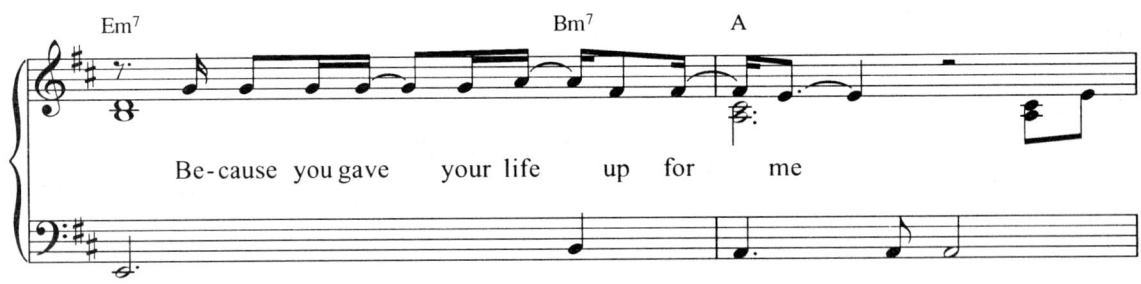

Be - cause you gave your life up for me

I will ne - ver be the same. You are so

© Copyright 2001 Kevin Mayhew Ltd.

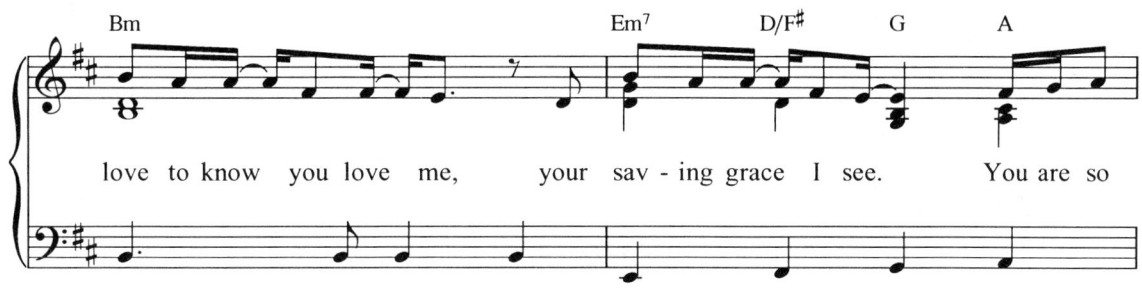
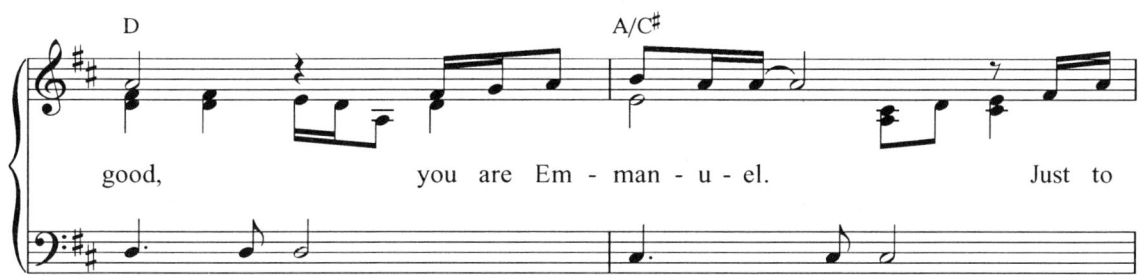
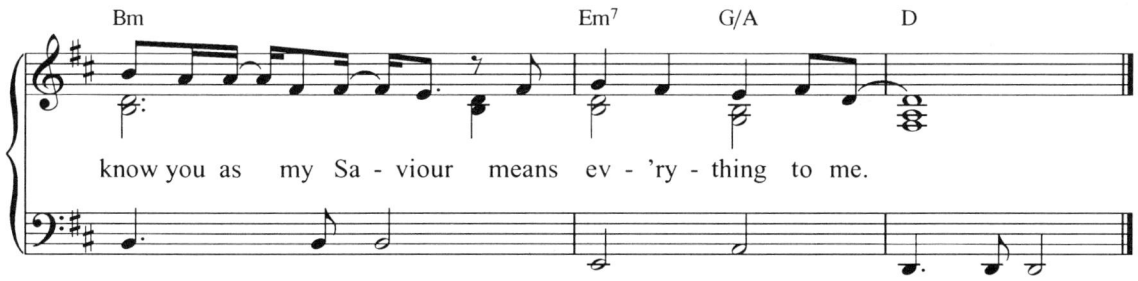

2. Jesus, I have come to wonder
   at the beauty of your name.
   And as I live each moment for you
   I will never be the same.

103 King of kings, majesty

Words and Music: Jarrod Cooper

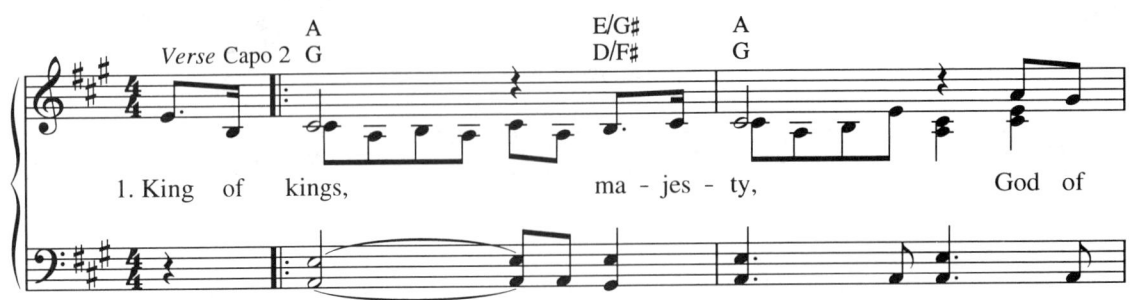
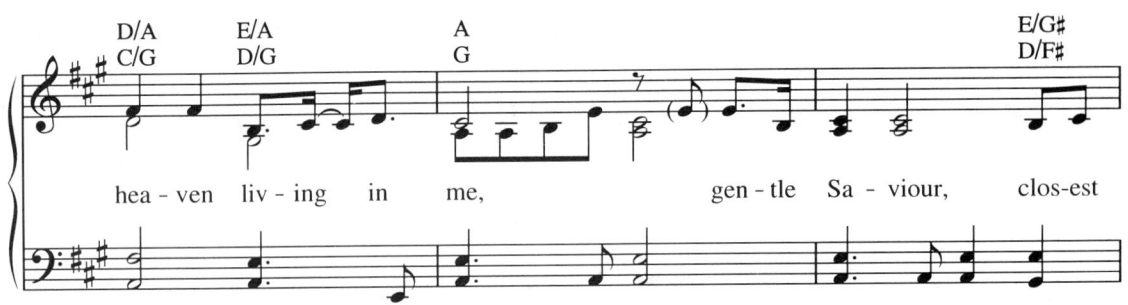

© Copyright 1998 Sovereign Lifestyle Music Ltd. P.O. Box 356,
Leighton Buzzard, Bedfordshire, LU7 3WP. Used by permission.

2. Earth and heav'n worship you,
   love eternal, faithful and true,
   who bought the nations, ransomed souls,
   brought this sinner near to your throne;
   all within me cries out in praise.

104 King of love

Words and Music: Doug Horley
arr. Dave Bankhead

© Copyright 1999 Thankyou Music/Adm. by worshiptogether.com songs excl. UK & Europe, adm. by Kingsway Music. (tym@kingsway.co.uk). Used by permission.

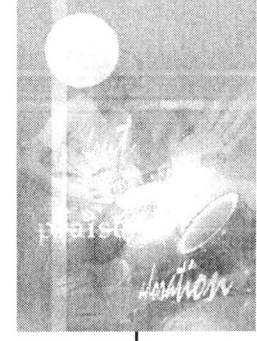

105 Lamb of God

Words and Music: Chris Bowater

Worshipfully

Lamb of God, Holy One, Jesus Christ, Son of God, lifted up willingly to die; that I the guilty one may know the blood once shed still freely flowing, still

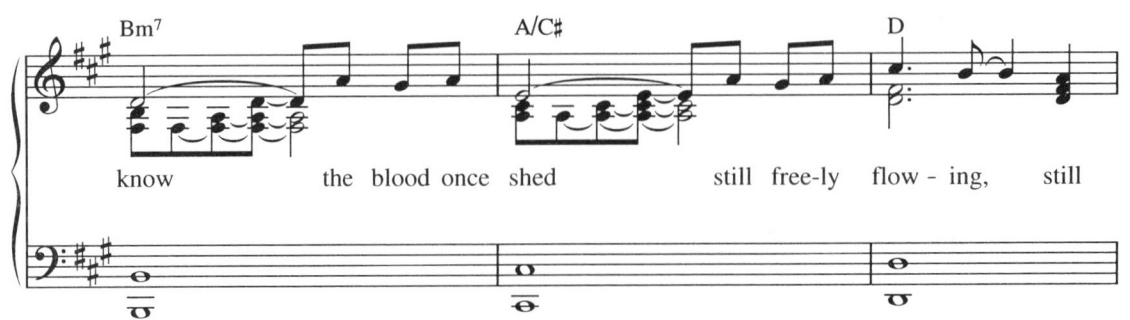

© Copyright 1988 Sovereign Lifestyle Music Ltd, P.O. Box 356,
Leighton Buzzard, Bedfordshire, LU7 3WP, UK. Used by permission.

106 Lead me, Lord

Words and Music: James Lewis

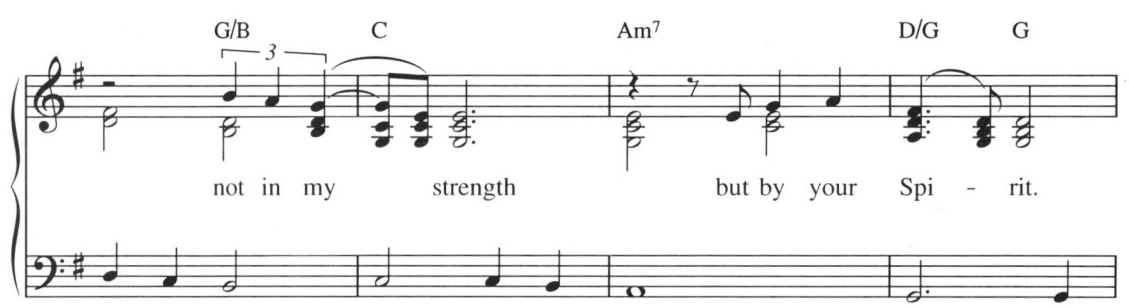

© Copyright 1999 Kevin Mayhew Ltd.

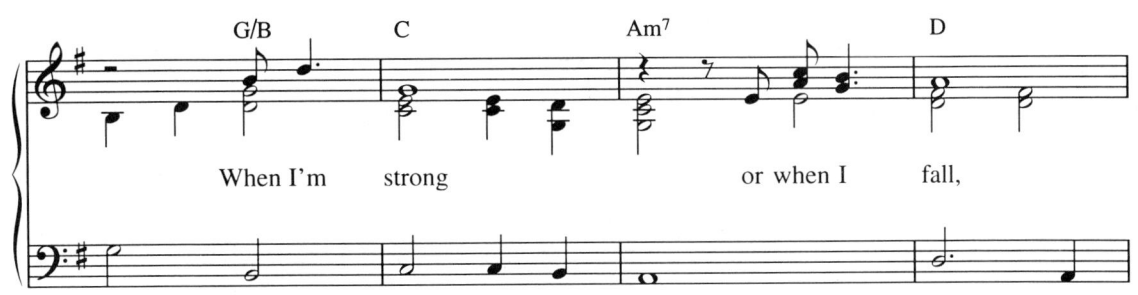

2. Praise you in the heavens,
   joining with the angels,
   joining you for ever and a day.
   Praise you on the earth now,
   joining with creation,
   calling all the nations to your praise.
   If they could see . . .

108 Light of the World

Words and Music: Tim Hughes

109 Living under the shadow of his wing

Words and Music: David Hadden and Bob Silvester

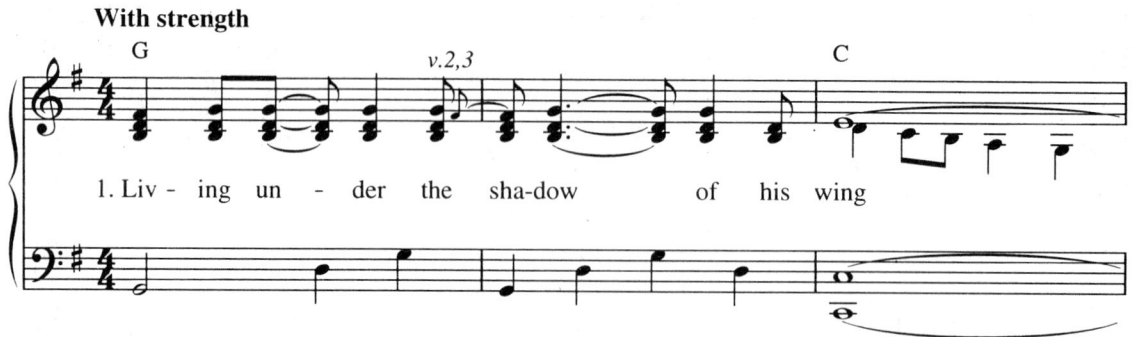

© Copyright 1983 Restoration Music Ltd. Administered by Sovereign Music UK,
P.O. Box 356, Leighton Buzzard, Bedfordshire, LU7 3WP, UK. Used by permission.

wor - ship to the King.

2. Bowed in adoration at his feet
   we dwell in harmony.
   Voices joined together that repeat,
   worthy, worthy, worthy is the Lamb.

3. Heart to heart embracing in his love
   reveals his purity.
   Soaring in my spirit like a dove,
   holy, holy, holy is the Lord.

110 Lord, for the years
Lord of the years

Words: Timothy Dudley-Smith
Music: Michael Baughen arr. David Iliff

LORD OF THE YEARS 11 10 11 10

1. Lord, for the years your love has kept and guided, urged and inspired us, cheered us on our way, sought us and saved us, pardon'd and provided, Lord of the years, we bring our thanks today.

2. Lord, for that word, the word of life which fires us, speaks to our hearts and sets our souls ablaze, teaches and trains, rebukes us and inspires us: Lord of the word, receive your people's praise.

3. Lord, for our land, in this our generation, spirits oppressed by pleasure, wealth and care; for young and old, for commonwealth and nation, Lord of our land, be pleased to hear our prayer.

4. Lord, for our world; when we disown and doubt you, loveless in strength, and comfortless in pain, hungry and helpless, lost indeed without you: Lord of the world, we pray that Christ may reign.

5. Lord, for ourselves; in living pow'r remake us – self on the cross and Christ upon the throne, past put behind us, for the future take us, Lord of our lives, to live for Christ alone.

Text © Copyright Timothy Dudley-Smith in Europe (including UK and Ireland) and in all territories not controlled by Hope Publishing Company.
Music © Copyright Michael Baughen/Jubilate Hymns, arrangement © Copyright David Iliff / Jubilate Hymns, 4 Thorne Park Road, Chelston, Torquay, Devon, TQ2 6RX. Used by permission.

111 Lord, let your glory fall

Words and Music: Matt Redman

© Copyright 1998 Thankyou Music/Adm. by worshiptogether.com songs excl. UK & Europe, adm. by Kingsway Music. (tym@kingsway.co.uk). Used by permission.

2. Voices in unison
   giving you thanks and praise,
   joined by the instruments,
   and then your glory came.
   Your presence like a cloud
   upon that ancient day,
   the priests were overwhelmed
   because your glory came.

3. A sacrifice was made,
   and then your fire came;
   they knelt upon the ground,
   and with one voice they praised.
   A sacrifice was made,
   and then your fire came;
   they knelt upon the ground,
   and with one voice they praised.

112 Lord of glory, we adore you

Words: R. Holden
revised and adapted by Graham Kendrick

Music: Henry John Gauntlett

IRBY 87 87 77

2. Mighty King in heav'n exalted,
   rightful heir and Lord of all,
   once despised, disowned, rejected
   by the ones you came to call;
   you we honour, you adore,
   glorious now and evermore.

3. Lord of life, to death made subject,
   blesser, yet a curse once-made
   of your Father's heart the object,
   yet in depths of anguish laid;
   you we gaze on, you recall,
   bearing here our sorrows all.

© Copyright 2001 Make Way Music, P.O. Box 263, Croydon, Surrey CR9 5AP, UK.
International copyright secured. All rights reserved. Used by permission.

113 Lord, the light of your love
Shine, Jesus, shine

Words and Music: Graham Kendrick

© Copyright 1987 Make Way Music, P.O. Box 263, Croydon, Surrey, CR9 5AP, UK.
International copyright secured. All rights reserved. Used by permission.

2. Lord, I come to your awesome presence,
   from the shadows into your radiance;
   by the blood I may enter your brightness,
   search me, try me, consume all my darkness.
   Shine on me, shine on me.

3. As we gaze on your kingly brightness,
   so our faces display your likeness,
   ever changing from glory to glory;
   mirrored here may our lives tell your story.
   Shine on me, shine on me.

   (Chorus twice to end)

114 Lord, we long to see your glory

Words and Music: Richard Lewis

116 Lord, you are so precious to me

Words and Music: Graham Kendrick

Lord, you are so gracious to me . . .
Lord, you are a father to me . . .
Lord, you are so faithful to me . . .
Lord, you are so loving to me . . .

© Copyright 1986 Thankyou Music/Adm. by worshiptogether.com songs excl. UK & Europe, adm. by Kingsway Music. (tym@kingsway.co.uk). Used by permission.

118 Lord, you put a tongue in my mouth

Words and Music: Ian Smale

© Copyright 1983 Thankyou Music/Adm. by worshiptogether.com songs excl. UK & Europe, adm. by Kingsway Music. (tym@kingsway.co.uk). Used by permission.

2. Lord, you put some hands on my arms
   which I want to raise to you . . . *etc.*

3. Lord, you put some feet on my legs
   and I want to dance to you . . . *etc.*

119 Lord, you've been good to me

Words and Music: Graham Kendrick
arr. Richard Lewis

1. Lord, you've been good to me all my life,
2. So may each breath I take be for you, Lord,

all my life; your loving kindness never fails.
only you, giving you back the life I owe.

I will re-
Love so a-

member all you have done, bring from my
mazing, mercy so free, Lord, you've been

© Copyright 2001 Make Way Music, P.O. Box 263, Croydon, Surrey CR9 5AP, UK.
International copyright secured. All rights reserved. Used by permission.

120 Love songs from heaven

Words and Music: Noel and Tricia Richards

1. Love songs from heaven are filling the earth,

bringing great hope to all nations;

evil has prospered, but truth is alive,

in this dark world the light still shines.

D.C. for verse 2

© Copyright 1996 Thankyou Music/Adm. by worshiptogether.com songs excl. UK & Europe, adm. by Kingsway Music. (tym@kingsway.co.uk). Used by permission.

2. Nothing has silenced this gospel of Christ,
   it echoes down through the ages.
   Blood of the martyrs has made your Church strong,
   in this dark world the light still shines.

3. Let ev'ry nation be filled with your song;
   this is the cry of your people,
   'We will not settle for anything less,
   in this dark world our light must shine.'

121 Meekness and majesty
This is your God
Words and Music: Graham Kendrick

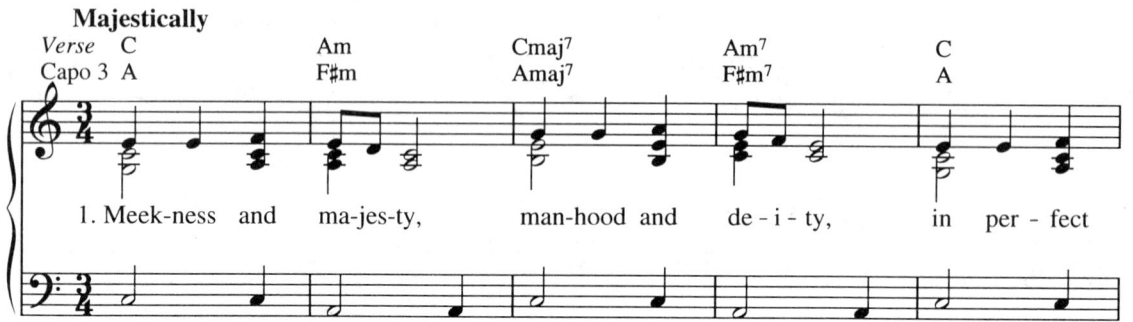

© Copyright 1986 Thankyou Music/Adm. by worshiptogether.com songs excl. UK & Europe, adm. by Kingsway Music. (tym@kingsway.co.uk). Used by permission.

2. Father's pure radiance,
   perfect in innocence,
   yet learns obedience
   to death on a cross.
   Suffering to give us life,
   conquering through sacrifice,
   and as they crucify
   prays: 'Father forgive.'

3. Wisdom unsearchable,
   God the invisible,
   love indestructible
   in frailty appears.
   Lord of infinity,
   stooping so tenderly,
   lifts our humanity
   to the heights of his throne.

122 Men of faith
Shout to the North
Words and Music: Martin Smith

© Copyright 1995 Curious? Music UK. PO Box 40, Arundel, West Sussex BN18 0UQ, UK. Used by permission.

2. Rise up, women of the truth,
   stand and sing to broken hearts.
   Who can know the healing pow'r
   of our awesome King of love?

3. Rise up, church with broken wings,
   fill this place with songs again
   of our God who reigns on high,
   by his grace again we'll fly.

123 Mercy and love

Words and Music: Chris Orange
arr. Chris Mitchell

1. Mercy and love, a pure offering,
2. Faithful and true, your word never ends.

you gave your life, freed me from sin.
Strength for the weak, life for the dead.

Let now the oil of this thankful heart
My great Redeemer, my closest friend, em-

flow out to you, my Lord.
pow'r me to live for

© Copyright 2001 Kevin Mayhew Ltd.

124 My first love
Like a child
Words and Music: Stuart Townend

© Copyright 1996 Thankyou Music/Adm. by worshiptogether.com songs excl. UK & Europe, adm. by Kingsway Music. (tym@kingsway.co.uk). Used by permission.

2. My first love is a rushing river,
   a waterfall that will never cease;
   and in the torrent of tears and laughter,
   I feel a healing power released.
   And I will draw from your well of life, my love.
   And in your grace I'll be satisfied, my love.

3. Restore the years of the church's slumber,
   revive the fire that has grown so dim;
   renew the love of those first encounters,
   that we may come alive again.
   And we will rise like the dawn throughout the earth,
   until the trumpet announces your return.

125 My heart is full
All the glory
Words and Music: Graham Kendrick

© Copyright 1991 Make Way Music, P.O. Box 263, Croydon, Surrey, CR9 5AP, UK.
International copyright secured. All rights reserved. Used by permission.

2. *(Men)* You love what's right and hate what's evil,
   therefore your God sets you on high,
   (Women) and on your head pours oil of gladness,
   while fragrance fills your royal palaces.

3. *(All)* Your throne, O God, will last for ever,
   justice will be your royal decree.
   In majesty, ride out victorious,
   for righteousness, truth and humility.

126 My lips shall praise you
Restorer of my soul

Words and Music: Noel and Tricia Richards

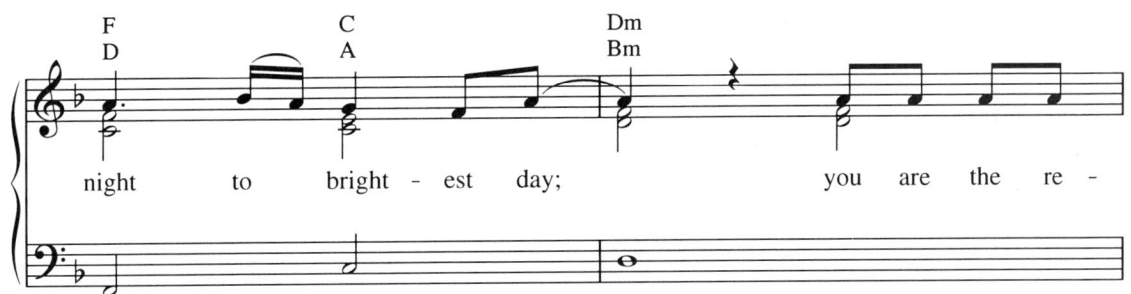

2. Love that conquers ev'ry fear,
   in the midst of trouble you draw near;
   you are the restorer of my soul.

3. You're the source of happiness,
   bringing peace when I am in distress;
   you are the restorer of my soul.

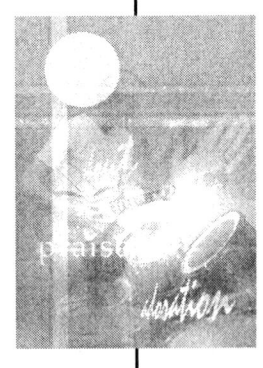

127 My Lord, I come to honour you
My Redeemer lives

Words and Music: Chris Orange
arr. Richard Lewis

© Copyright 2001 Kevin Mayhew Ltd.

128 My Lord, what love is this
Amazing love
Words and Music: Graham Kendrick

© Copyright 1989 Make Way Music, P.O. Box 263, Croydon, Surrey, CR9 5AP, UK.
International copyright secured. All rights reserved. Used by permission.

2. And so they watched him die,
   despised, rejected;
   but O, the blood he shed
   flowed for me!

3. And now this love of Christ
   shall flow like rivers;
   come, wash your guilt away,
   live again!

129 No scenes of stately majesty

Words and Music: Graham Kendrick

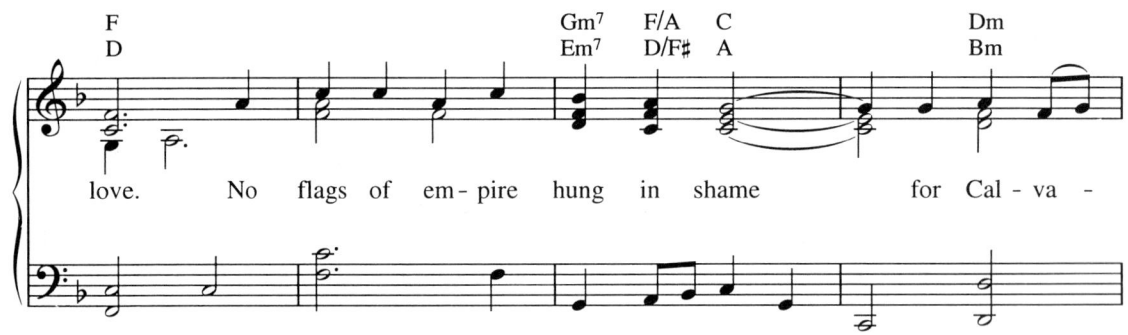
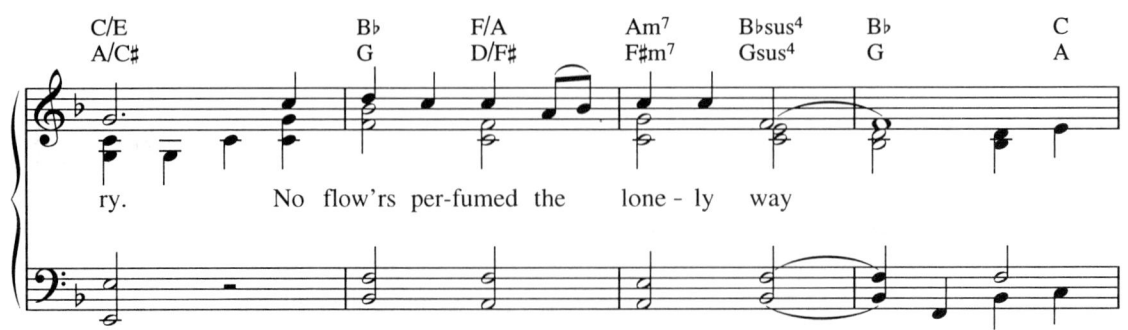

© Copyright 1997 Make Way Music,
P.O. Box 263, Croydon, Surrey, CR9 5AP, UK. Used by permission.

2. No wreaths upon the ground were laid
   for the King of kings.
   only a crown of thorns remained
   where he gave his love.
   A message scrawled in irony –
   King of the Jews –
   lay trampled where they turned away,
   and no-one knew
   that it was the first Easter Day.

3. Yet nature's finest colours blaze
   for the King of kings.
   And stars in jewelled clusters say,
   'Worship heaven's King.'
   Two thousand springtimes more have bloomed –
   is that enough?
   Oh, how can I be satisfied
   until he hears
   the whole world sing of Easter love.

4. My prayers shall be a fragrance sweet
   for the King of kings.
   My love the flowers at his feet
   for the King of love.
   My vigil is to watch and pray
   until he comes.
   My highest tribute to obey
   and live to know
   the power of that first Easter Day.

5. I long for scenes of majesty
   for the risen King.
   or nights aglow with candle flame
   for the King of love.
   A nation hushed upon its knees
   at Calvary,
   where all our sins and griefs were nailed
   and hope was born
   of everlasting Easter Day.

130 Not by might

Words and Music: Robin Mark

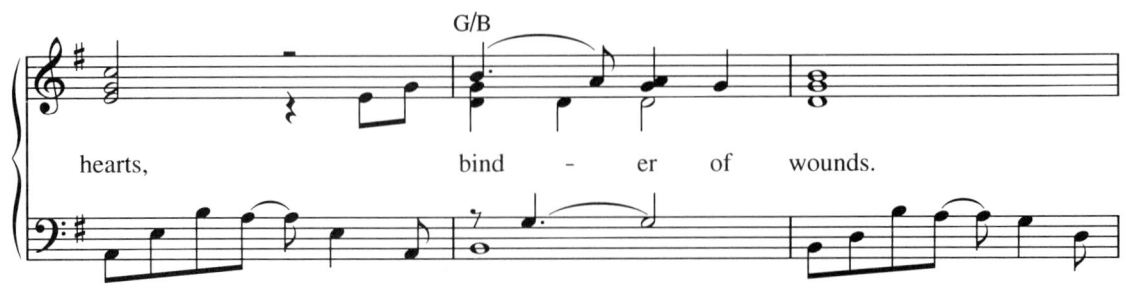

© Copyright 1996 Daybreak Music, PO Box 2848 Eastbourne, BN20 7XP. All rights reserved.
(info@daybreakmusic.co.uk). International Copyright Secured. Used by permission.

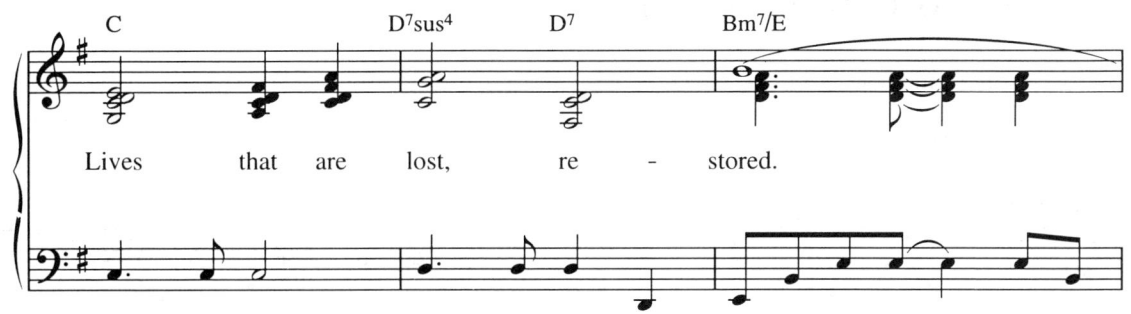
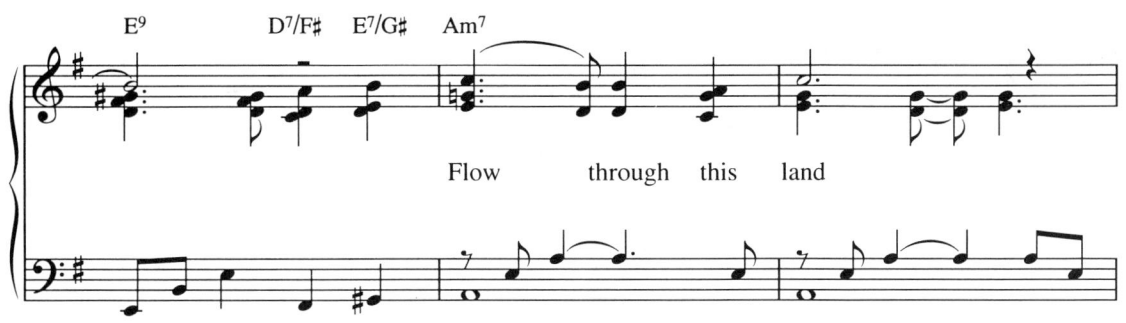

131 Nothing in this world

Words and Music: Tim Hughes

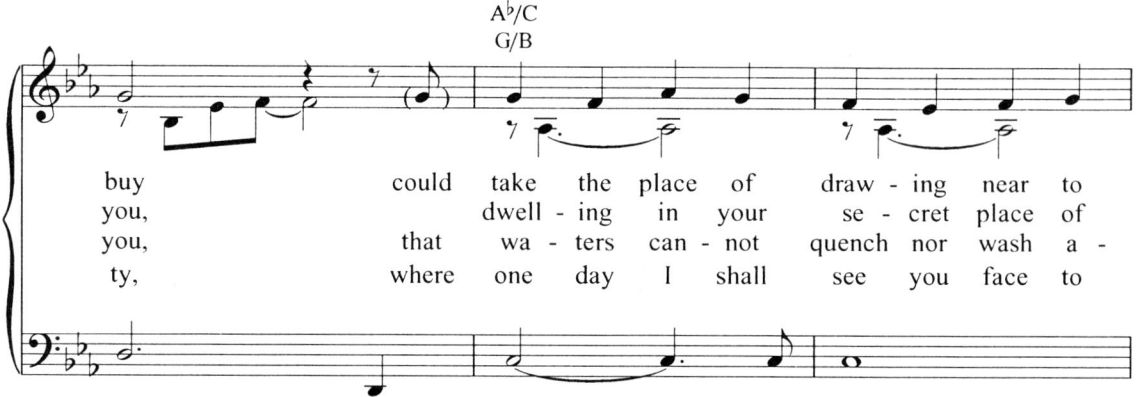

© Copyright 1998 Thankyou Music/Adm. by worshiptogether.com songs excl. UK & Europe, adm. by Kingsway Music. (tym@kingsway.co.uk). Used by permission.

132 Nothing shall separate us

Words and Music: Noel and Tricia Richards

© Copyright 1989 Thankyou Music/Adm. by worshiptogether.com songs excl. UK & Europe, adm. by Kingsway Music. (tym@kingsway.co.uk) Used by permission.

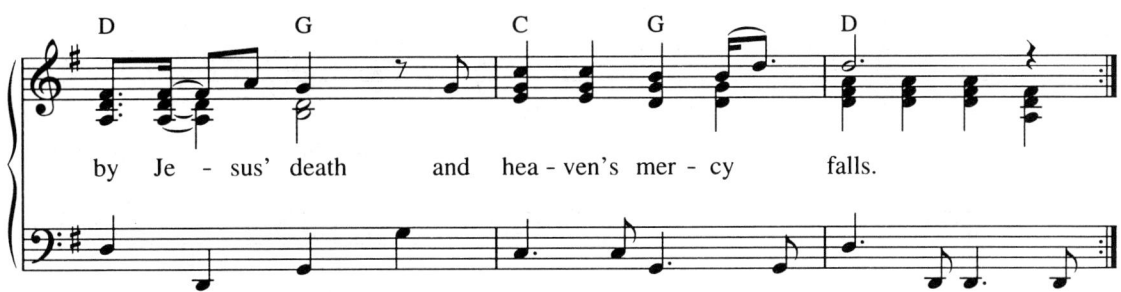

2. Up from the grave Jesus was raised
   to sit at God's right hand;
   pleading our cause in heaven's courts,
   forgiven we can stand.

3. Now by God's grace we have embraced
   a life set free from sin;
   we shall deny all that destroys
   our union with him.

133 O Father of the fatherless
Father me

Words and Music: Graham Kendrick

2. When bruised and broken I draw near,
   you hold me close and dry my tears;
   I love the way you father me.
   At last my fearful heart is still,
   surrendered to your perfect will;
   I love the way you father me.

3. If in my foolishness I stray,
   returning empty and ashamed,
   I love the way you father me.
   Exchanging for my wretchedness
   your radiant robes of righteousness,
   I love the way you father me.

4. And when I look into your eyes,
   from deep within my spirit cries,
   I love the way you father me.
   Before such love I stand amazed
   and ever will through endless days;
   I love the way you father me.

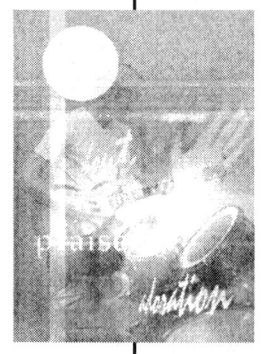

134 O God of love
How good it is

Words and Music: Louise and Nathan Fellingham

1. O God of love, I come to you again,
   knowing I'll find mercy.
2. O God of strength, your hand is on my life,
   bringing peace to me.

I can't explain all the things I see,
You know my frame, you know how I am made,

but I'll trust in you.   In
you planned all my days.

© Copyright 2000 Thankyou Music/Adm. by worshiptogether.com songs excl. UK & Europe,
adm. by Kingsway Music. (tym@kingsway.co.uk). Used by permission.

135 Oh, lead me

Words and Music: Martin Smith

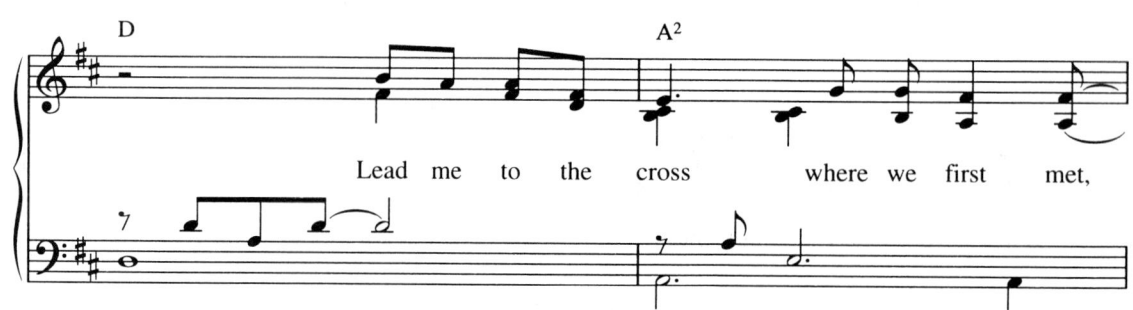

© Copyright 1994 Curious? Music UK. PO Box 40, Arundel, West Sussex BN18 0UQ, UK.
Used by permission.

136 O Jesus, Son of God
Light of the world

Words and Music: Matt Redman

1. O Jesus, Son of God, so full of grace and truth, the Father's saving Word: so wonderful are you.
2. In you all things were made, and nothing without you, in heaven and on earth, all things are held in you.

The angels long to see, and prophets search to find
your birth was prophesied, for you were the Messiah,
And yet you became flesh, living as one of us,

© Copyright 2000 Thankyou Music/Adm. by worshiptogether.com songs excl. UK & Europe, adm. by Kingsway Music. (tym@kingsway.co.uk). Used by permission.

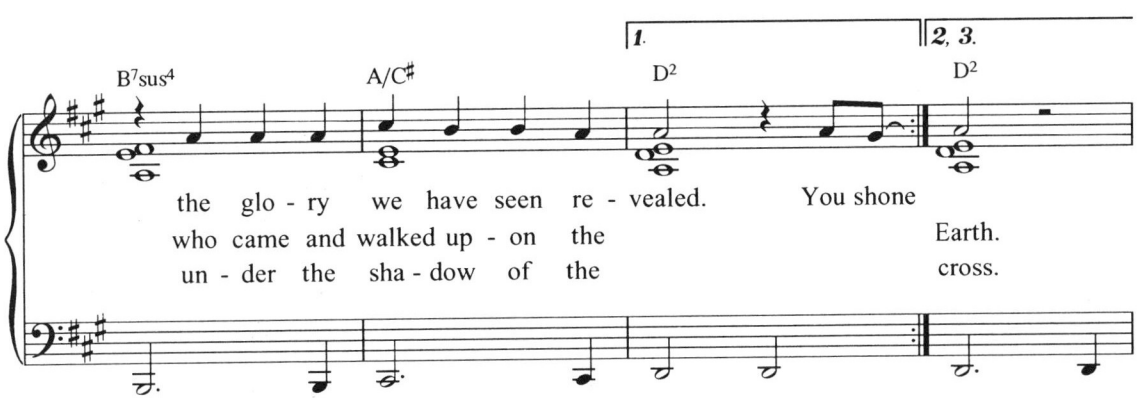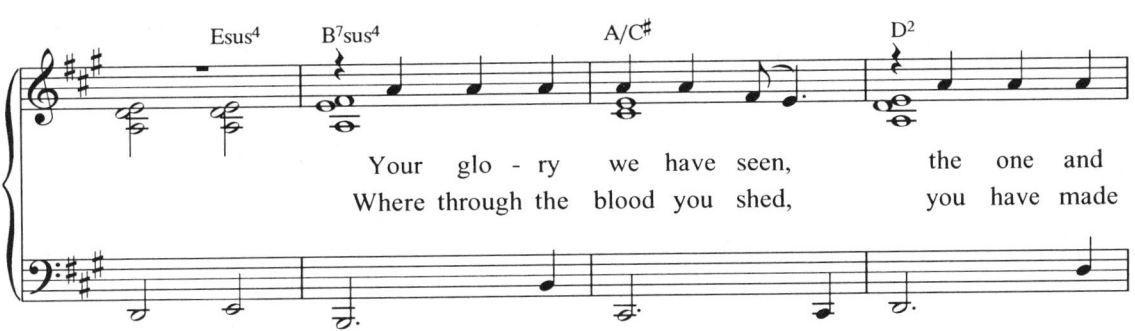

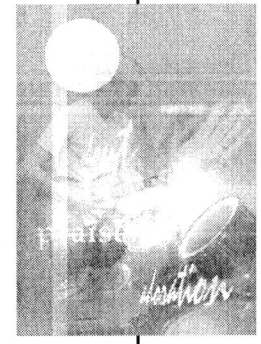

137 O Lord our God
We will magnify
Words and Music: Philip Lawson Johnston

© Copyright 1982 Thankyou Music/Adm. by worshiptogether.com songs excl. UK & Europe, adm. by Kingsway Music. (tym@kingsway.co.uk). Used by permission.

2. O Lord our God, you have established a throne,
   you reign in righteousness and splendour.
   O Lord our God, the skies are ringing with your praise;
   soon those on earth will come to worship.

3. O Lord our God, the world was made at your command,
   in you all things now hold together.
   Now to him who sits on the throne and to the Lamb
   be praise and glory and pow'r for ever.

138 O Lord, your tenderness

Words and Music: Graham Kendrick

© Copyright 1986 Thankyou Music/Adm. by worshiptogeter.com songs excl. UK & Europe, adm. by Kingsway Music. (tym@kingsway.co.uk). Used by permission.

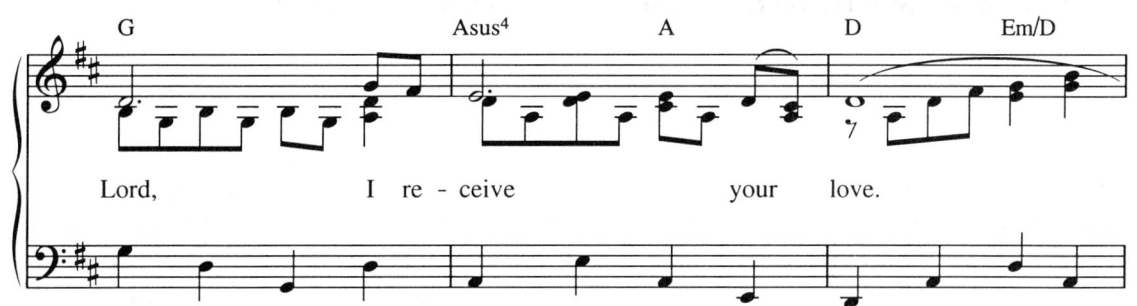

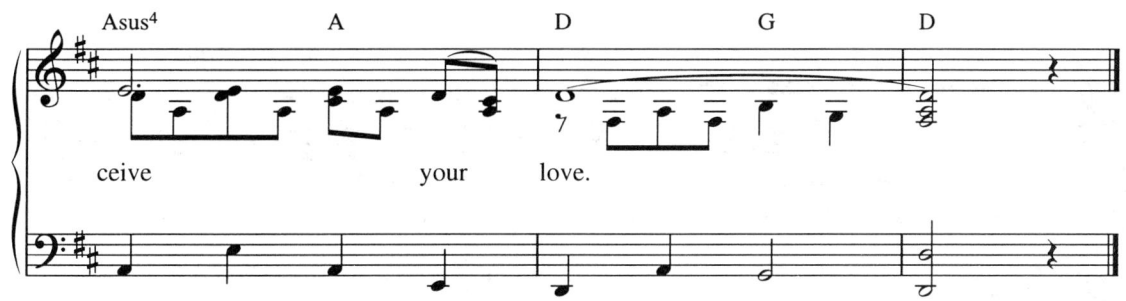

139 O my soul, arise and bless your maker

Words and Music: Stuart Townend

2. King of grace, his love is overwhelming,
   bread of life, he's all I'll ever need.
   For his blood has purchased me for ever,
   bought at the cross of Jesus.

3. When I wake, I know that he is with me,
   when I'm weak, I know that he is strong.
   Though I fall, his arm is there to lean on,
   safe on the rock of Jesus.

4. Stir in me the songs that you are singing,
   fill my gaze with things as yet unseen.
   Give me faith to move in works of power,
   making me more like Jesus.

5. Then one day, I'll see him as he sees me,
   face to face, the lover and the loved.
   No more words, the longing will be over,
   there with my precious Jesus.

140 One Lord, one faith
Increase in me

Words and Music: Steve Thompson, Velveta Thompson and Andy Mitchell

1. One Lord, one faith, we stand to-geth-er,

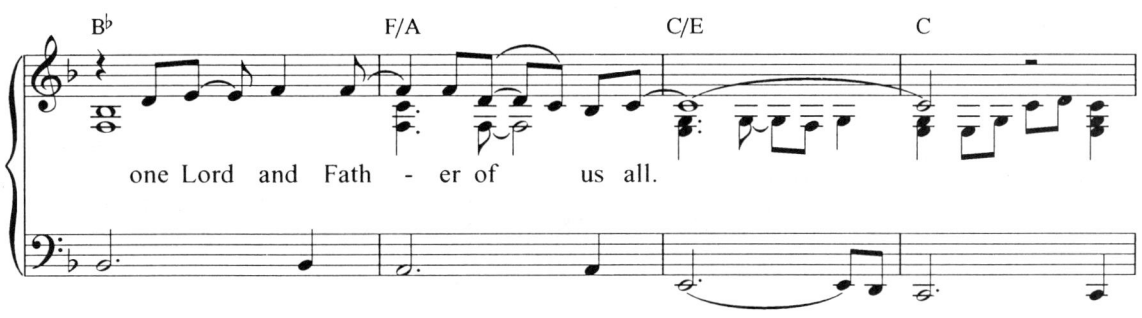

one Lord and Fath-er of us all.

In u-ni-ty and by God's Spi-rit,

we walk as one to reach our goal.

© 1999 Beracah Music, 61 Penny Hill Drive, Clayton, Bradford, W Yorks BD14 6NH.

2. To reach the lost is our commission;
to stretch our hands to those in need.
Reflect God's heart, fulfil his calling,
and then his kingdom will increase.

141 On the blood-stained ground
I kneel down

Words and Music: Graham Kendrick

© Copyright 1998 Ascent Music, P.O. Box 263, Croydon, Surrey CR9 5AP, UK.
International copyright secured. All rights reserved. Used by permission.

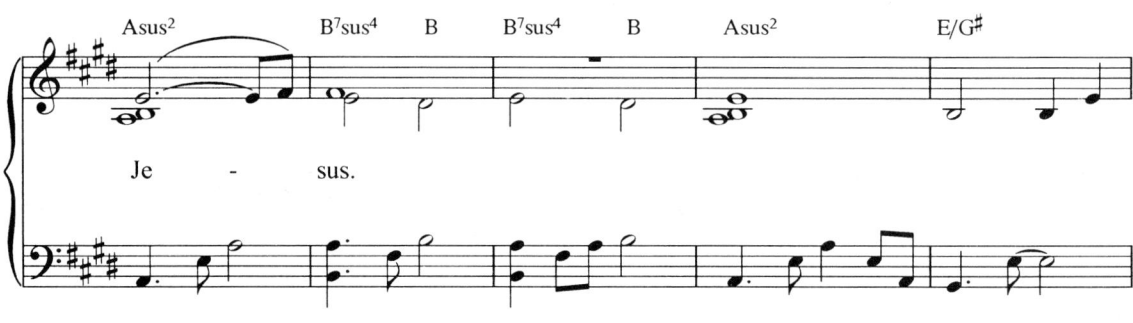

142 On the cross

Words and Music: Geoff Baker

© Copyright 1998 Daybreak Music Ltd., PO Box 2848, Eastbourne, BN20 7XP, UK.
All rights reserved. (info@daybreakmusic.co.uk). International copyright secured. Used by permission.

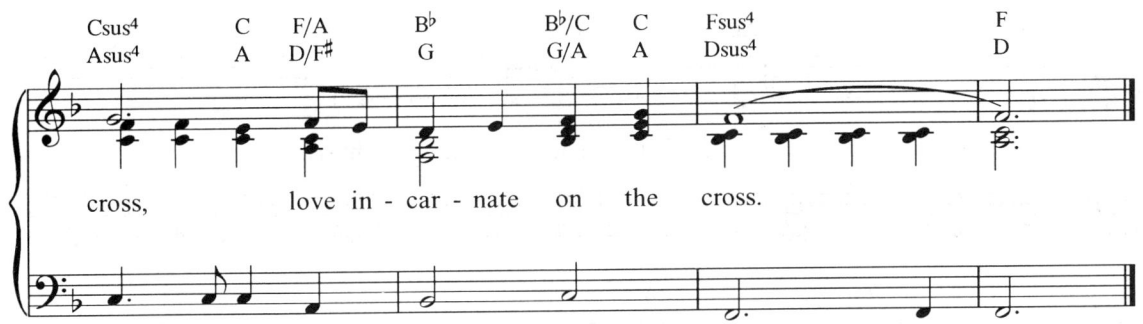

2. At the cross, at the cross,
   all my sin on Jesus laid.
   Mine the debt, his the cost,
   by his blood the price is paid.
   And through his suffering,
   that fragrant offering,
   arms of love are opened wide.
   At the cross, at the cross,
   there is healing at the cross.

3. To the cross, to the cross,
   Spirit lead me to the cross.
   Bowed in awe at his feet,
   richest gain I count as loss.
   Nothing compares with this,
   to share his righteousness
   and be called a child of God.
   To the cross, to the cross,
   Spirit lead me to the cross.

143 O sacred King

Words and Music: Matt Redman

© Copyright 1999 Thankyou Music/Adm. by worshiptogether.com songs excl. UK & Europe, adm. by Kingsway Music. (tym@kingsway.co.uk). Used by permission.

144 O, taste and see
Taste and see

Words and Music: Dave Bilbrough

© Copyright 1999 Thankyou Music/Adm. by worshiptogether.com songs excl. UK & Europe,
adm. by Kingsway Music. (tym@kingsway.co.uk). Used by permission.

145 O the blood of my Saviour

Words and Music: Colin Owen

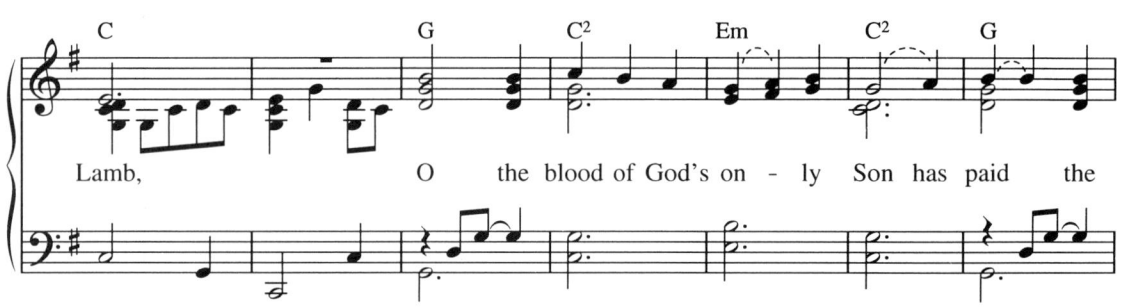

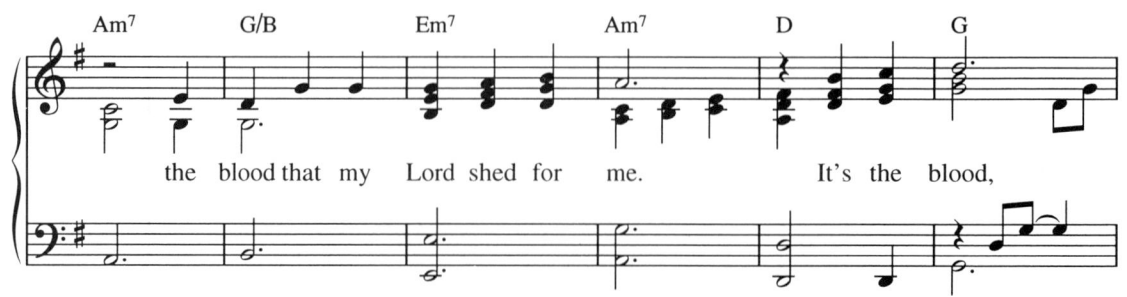

© Copyright 1993 Thankyou Music/Adm. by worshiptogether.com songs excl. UK & Europe, adm. by Kingsway Music. (tym@kingsway.co.uk). Used by permission.

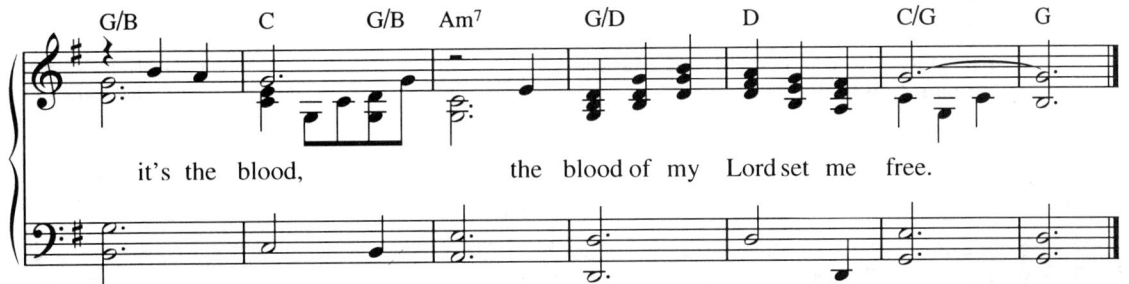

2. O the blood shed at Calv'ry,
   O the blood spilled for me,
   O the blood of God's only Son,
   Jesus, your blood set me free.

3. O the blood from the nail prints,
   O the blood from the thorns,
   O the blood from the spear in his side
   has given me life evermore.

146 O, the love of God is boundless

Words: D.R. Edwards, revised and adapted
by Graham Kendrick

Music: Graham Kendrick
arr. Richard Lewis

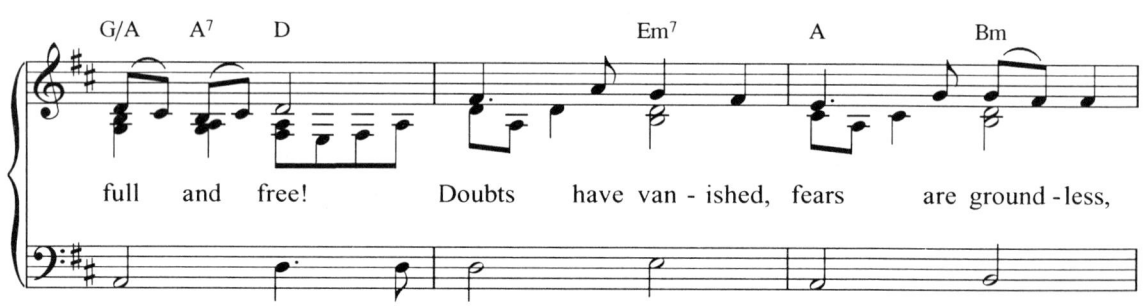

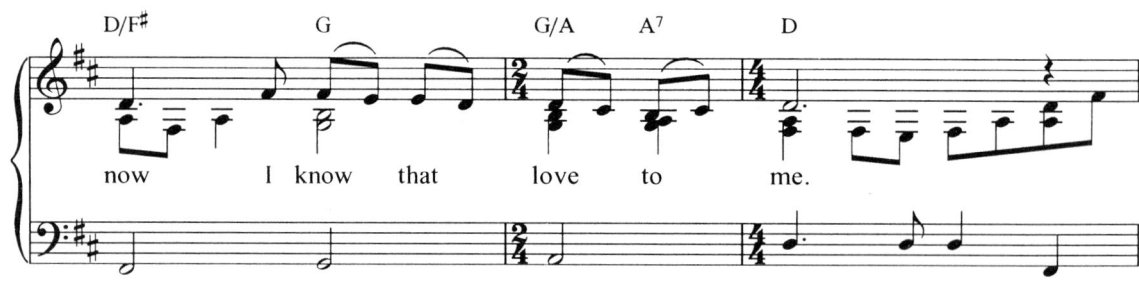

Words (this version) and melody © Copyright 2001 Make Way Music, PO Box 263, Croydon,
Surrey CR9 5AP, UK. International copyright secured. All rights reserved. Used by permission.

2. O, the cross of Christ is wondrous!
   There I learn God's heart to me
   'midst the silent, deep'ning darkness
   'God is light' I also see.
   Holy claims of justice finding
   full expression in that scene;
   light and love alike are telling
   what his woe and suff'ring means.

3. O, the sight of heav'n is glorious!
   Man in righteousness is there.
   Once the victim, now victorious,
   Jesus lives in glory fair!
   Him, who met the claims of glory
   and the need of ruined man
   on the cross, O wondrous story!
   God has set at his right hand.

4. O, what rest of soul in seeing
   Jesus on his Father's throne!
   Yes, what peace for everflowing
   from God's rest in his own Son!
   Gazing upward into heaven,
   reading glory in his face,
   knowing that 'tis he, once given
   on the cross to take my place.

147 Our confidence is in the Lord

Words and Music: Noel and Tricia Richards

© Copyright 1989 Thankyou Music/Adm. by worshiptogether.com songs excl. UK & Europe, adm. by Kingsway Music. (tym@kingsway.co.uk). Used by permission.

148 Our God is great

Words and Music: Dave Bilbrough

© Copyright 1996 Thankyou Music/Adm. by worshiptogether.com songs excl. UK & Europe, adm. by Kingsway Music. (tym@kingsway.co.uk). Used by permission.

149 Over the mountains and the sea
I could sing of your love for ever

Words and Music: Martin Smith

© Copyright 1994 Curious? Music UK. PO Box 40, Arundel, West Sussex BN18 0UQ, UK.
Used by permission.

150 Praise God from whom all blessings flow

Words and Music: Andy Piercy and Dave Clifton arr. Alison Berry

© Copyright 1993 IQ Music Limited (for the world), Orchard House, Broad Street, Tylers Green, Cuckfield, West Sussex, RH17 5DZ, UK. Used by permission.

151 Praise the Lord

Words and Music: Tim Lomax

© Copyright 1999 Kevin Mayhew Ltd.

2. Praise him, sun, praise him, moon.
   Praise him, all you bright stars,
   praise him, all you highest heav'ns.
   All you deepest oceans,
   come and praise the Lord.

152 Rain down

Words and Music: Richard Lewis

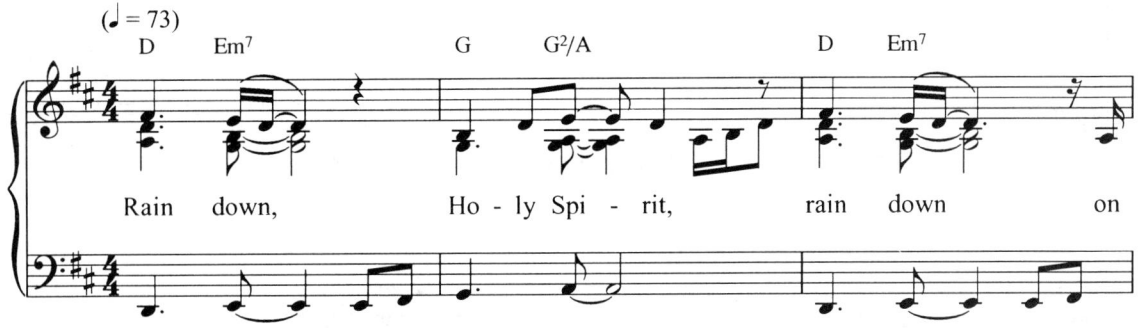

Rain down, Holy Spirit, rain down on

this thirsty land. We need your love, we need your pow'r, we

need a touch from your hand this hour. We cry for more of you,

Holy Spirit, rain down.

© Copyright 2001 Kevin Mayhew Ltd.

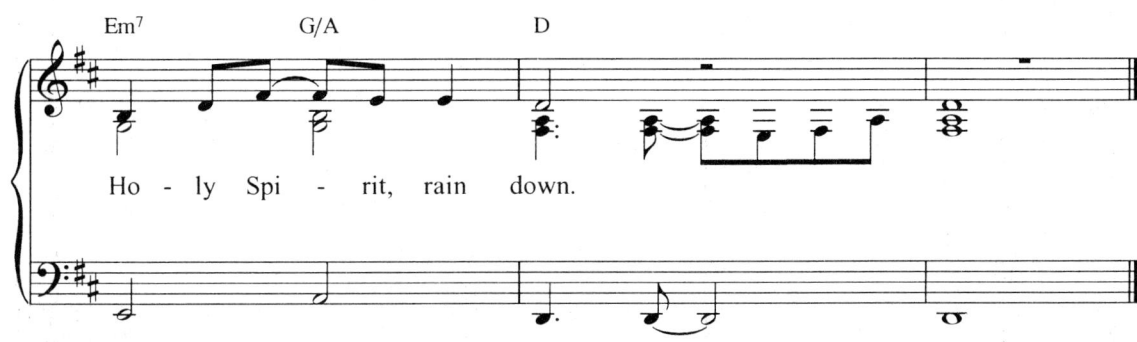

153 Reign in me

Words and Music: Chris Bowater

154 Rejoice!

Words and Music: Graham Kendrick

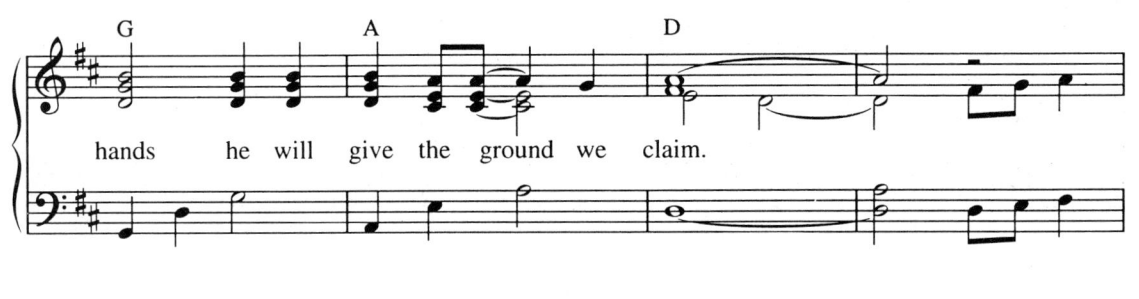
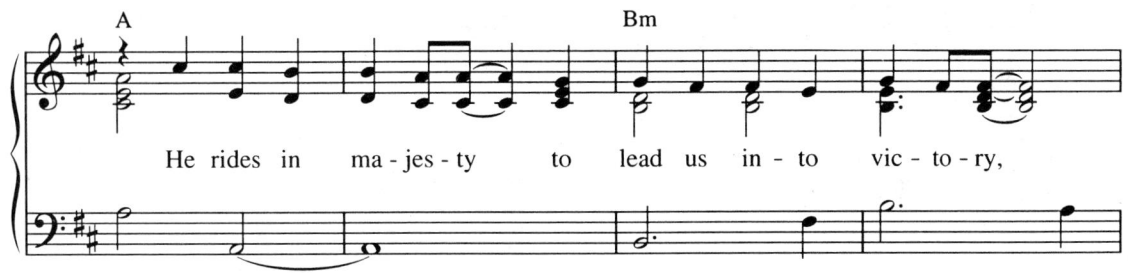

2. God is at work in us
   his purpose to perform,
   building a kingdom
   of power not of words,
   where things impossible
   by faith shall be made possible;
   let's give the glory to him now.

3. Though we are weak, his grace
   is ev'rything we need;
   we're made of clay
   but this treasure is within.
   He turns our weaknesses
   into his opportunities,
   so that the glory goes to him.

155 Restore, O Lord

Words and Music: Graham Kendrick and Chris Rolinson

2. Restore, O Lord,
in all the earth your fame,
and in our time revive
the church that bears your name.
And in your anger,
Lord, remember mercy,
O living God,
whose mercy shall outlast the years.

3. Bend us, O Lord,
where we are hard and cold,
in your refiner's fire:
come purify the gold.
Though suff'ring comes
and evil crouches near,
still our living God
is reigning, he is reigning here.

4. *as verse 1*

© Copyright 1981 Thankyou Music/Adm. by worshiptogether.com songs excl. UK & Europe,
adm. by Kingsway Music. (tym@kingsway.co.uk). Used by permission.

156 River, wash over me

Words and Music: Dougie Brown

Unhurried, with strength

1. River, wash over me, cleanse me and make me new.
Bathe me, refresh me and fill me anew.
River, wash over me.

2. Spirit, watch over me,
   lead me to Jesus' feet.
   Cause me to worship and fill me anew.
   Spirit, watch over me.

3. Jesus, rule over me,
   reign over all my heart.
   Teach me to praise you and fill me anew.
   Jesus, rule over me.

© Copyright 1980 Thankyou Music/Adm. by worshiptogether.com songs excl. UK & Europe, adm. by Kingsway Music. (tym@kingsway.co.uk). Used by permission.

157 Rock of ages

Words: Augustus Montague Toplady
revised and adapted by Graham Kendrick

Music: Graham Kendrick
arr. Richard Lewis

© Copyright 2001 Make Way Music, P.O. Box 263, Croydon, Surrey CR9 5AP, UK.
International copyright secured. All rights reserved. Used by permission.

2. Not the labours of my hands
can fulfil your law's demands.
Could my zeal no respite know,
could my tears for ever flow,
all for sin could not atone,
you must save and you alone.

3. Nothing in my hand I bring,
simply to your cross I cling.
Naked, come to you for dress,
helpless, look to you for grace.
Foul, I to the fountain fly,
wash me, Saviour, or I die.

4. While I draw this fleeting breath,
when my eyelids close in death,
when I soar to worlds unknown,
see you on your judgement throne,
Rock of ages, cleft for me,
let me hide myself in thee.

158 Salvation belongs to our God

Words and Music: Adrian Howard and Pat Turner

1. Sal-va-tion be-longs to our God, who

sits on the throne, and to the

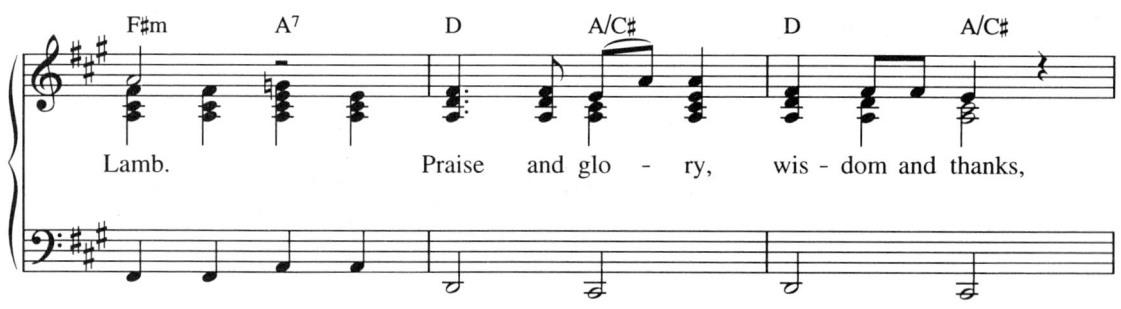
Lamb. Praise and glo-ry, wis-dom and thanks,

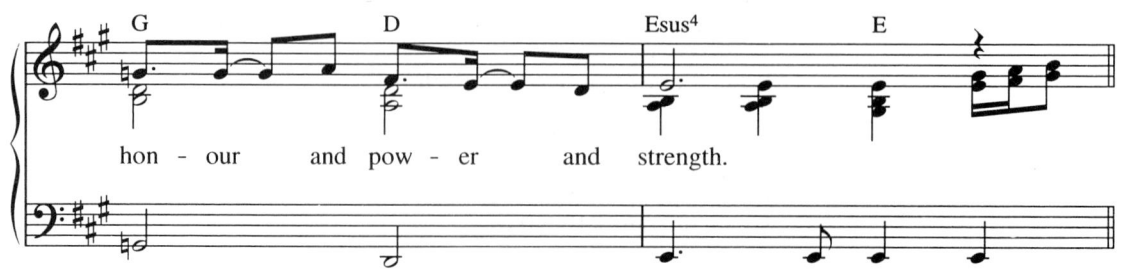
hon-our and pow-er and strength.

© Copyright 1985 Restoration Music Ltd. Administered by Sovereign Music UK,
PO Box 356, Leighton Buzzard, Bedfordshire, LU7 3WP, UK. Used by permission.

2. And we, the redeemed, shall be strong
   in purpose and unity,
   declaring aloud,
   praise and glory, wisdom and thanks,
   honour and power and strength.

159 Saviour, I will sing to you
Saviour of the world

Words and Music: Tim Lomax
arr. Richard Lewis

1. Sa-viour, I will sing to you a heart-felt song of love for
2. Je-sus, now you reach the lost in the sha-dow of the

you, and ev-'ry day I'll give my life
cross. It's there they taste your grace so sweet,

in wor-ship as a sac-ri-fice. You gave your all to set me
and there that love and jus-tice meet. You took the sting of death a-

free by dy-ing on the cross for me.
way and now we live in vic-to-ry.

© Copyright 2001 Kevin Mayhew Ltd.

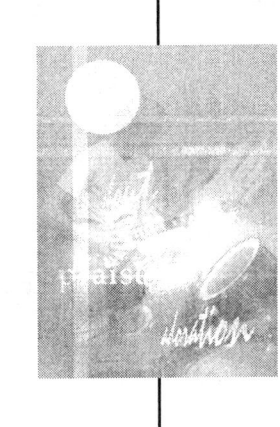

160 Shout for joy and sing

Words and Music: David Fellingham

161 Spirit of the Lord
Healing love

Words and Music: Ian White

Spi-rit of the Lord come down a-mong us now. Mi-ni-ster new life to bones grown dry. Some-thing in our heart cries out to be made whole, the touch of heal-ing love.

© Copyright 1994 Little Misty Music/Kingsway Music (tym@kingsway.co.uk).
Worldwide (excl. Australia & New Zealand). Used by permission.

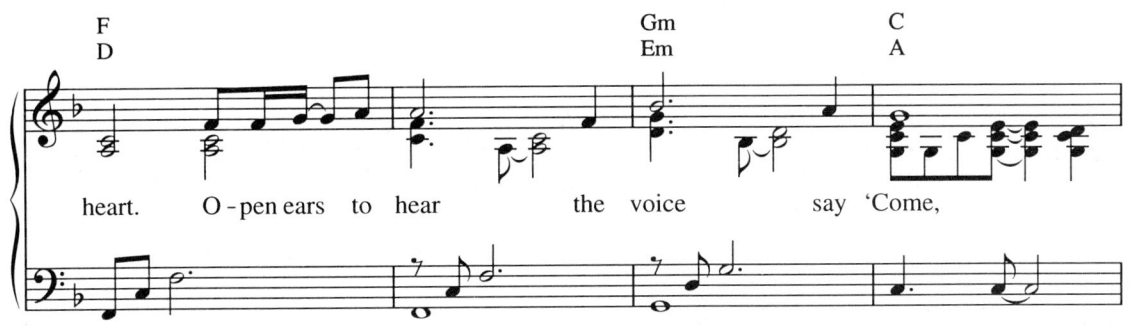

162 Such love

Words and Music: Graham Kendrick

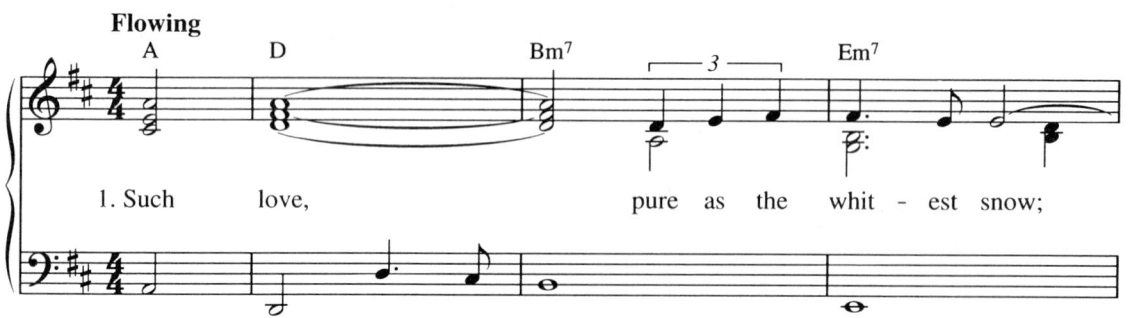

1. Such love, pure as the whitest snow;

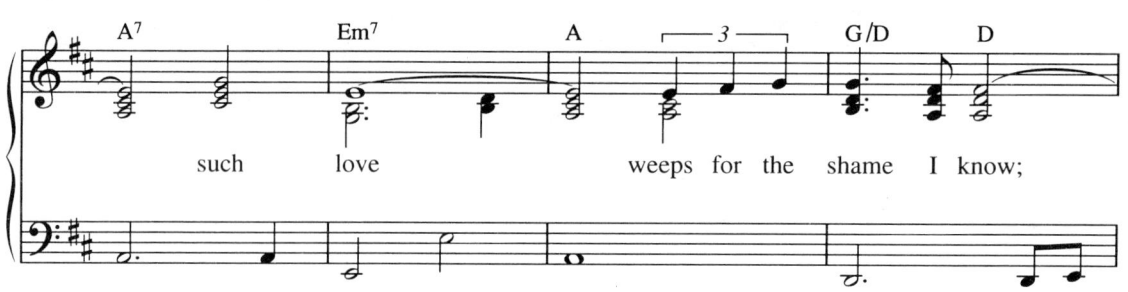

such love weeps for the shame I know;

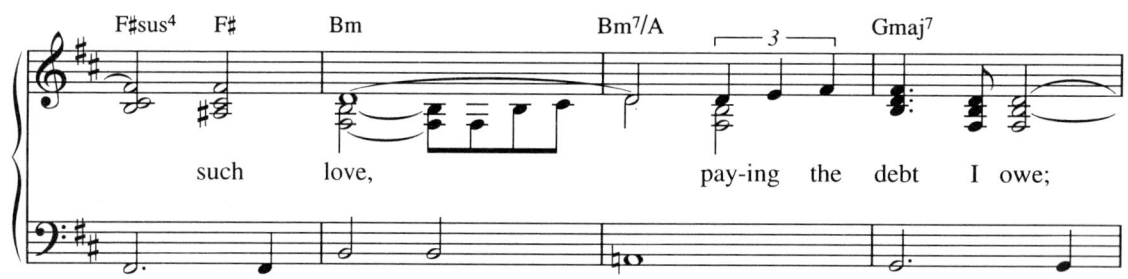

such love, paying the debt I owe;

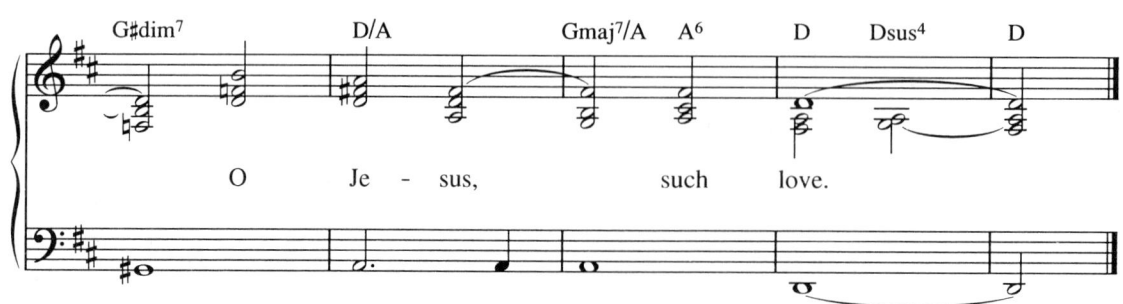

O Jesus, such love.

© Copyright 1988 Make Way Music, P.O. Box 263, Croydon, Surrey, CR9 5AP, UK.
International copyright secured. All rights reserved. Used by permission.

2. Such love, stilling my restlessness;
   such love, filling my emptiness;
   such love, showing me holiness;
   O Jesus, such love.

3. Such love springs from eternity;
   such love, streaming through history;
   such love, fountain of life to me;
   O Jesus, such love.

163 Surely our God
Revealer of mysteries
Words and Music: David and Liz Morris

© Copyright 1996 Tevita Music,
P.O. Box 46, Beckenham, Kent, BR3 4YR, UK. Used by permission.

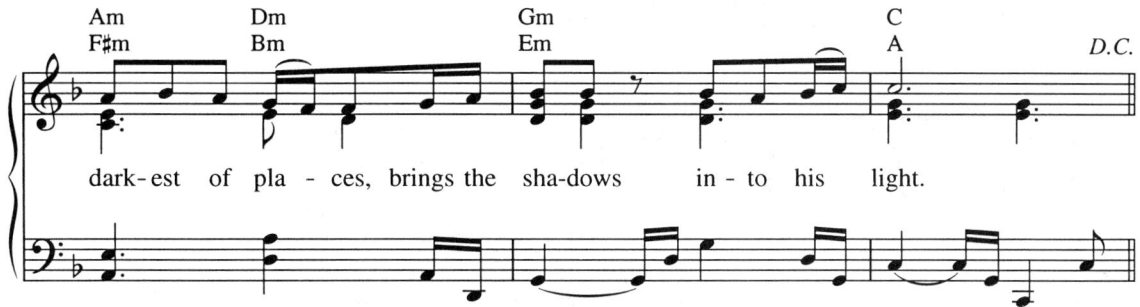

2. I will praise you always, my Father,
   you are Lord of heaven and earth,
   you hide your secrets from the wise and the learnèd
   and reveal them to this your child.

3. Thank you for sending your only Son,
   we may know the myst'ry of God;
   he opens the treasures of wisdom and knowledge
   to the humble, not to the proud.

164 Take us to the river

Words and Music: Robin Mark

© Copyright 1998 Thankyou Music/Adm. by worshiptogether.com songs excl. UK & Europe,
adm. by Kingsway Music. (tym@kingsway. co.uk). Used by permission.

2. Take us to your throne-room,
   give us ears to hear the cry of heaven;
   for that cry is mercy,
   mercy to the fallen sons of man:
   for mercy has triumphed.
   Triumphed over judgement by your blood;
   take us to the throne-room
   in the city of our God.

3. Take us to the mountain,
   lift us in the shadow of your hands;
   is this your mighty angel,
   who stands astride the ocean and the land?
   For in his hand your mercy
   showers on a dry and barren place;
   take us to the mountain
   in the city of our God.

2. Let all my movements express
   a heart that loves to say 'yes',
   a will that leaps to obey you.
   Let all my energy blaze
   to see the joy in your face;
   let my whole being praise you,
   praise you.

166 Tell the world

Words and Music: Dave Bilbrough

With an African feel

Chorus

Tell the world that Jesus is risen, let his praise en-

-circle the globe; make it known among all the nations that

Jesus is alive!

Verse

1. From the cradle to the grave, from a stable to a cross,

© Copyright 1998 Thankyou Music/Adm. by worshiptogether.com songs excl. UK & Europe,
adm. by Kingsway Music. (tym@kingsway.co.uk). Used by permission.

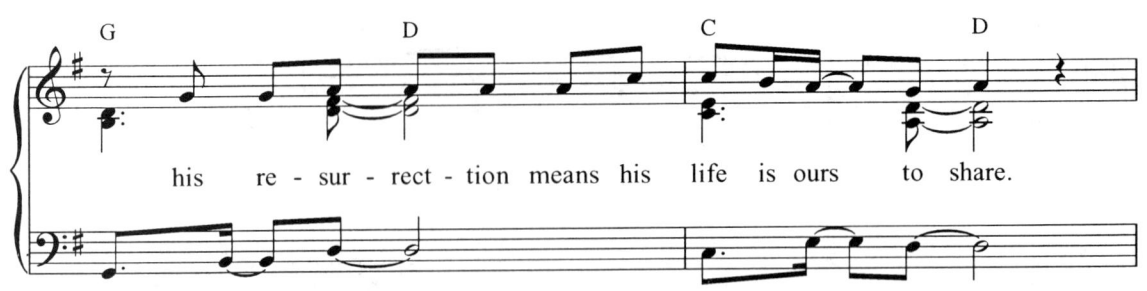

167 Thank you for saving me

Words and Music: Martin Smith

1. Thank you for saving me; what can I say?
You are my ev-'ry-thing, I will sing your praise.
You shed your blood for me; what can I say?
You took my sin and shame, a sinner called by name.

Great

© Copyright 1993 Curious? Music UK. PO Box 40, Arundel, West Sussex BN18 0UQ, UK.
Used by permission.

2. Mercy and grace are mine, forgiv'n is my sin;
   Jesus, my only hope, the Saviour of the world.
   'Great is the Lord,' we cry; God, let your kingdom come.
   Your word has let me see, thank you for saving me.

168 Thank you, thank you for the blood

Words and Music: Matt Redman

© Copyright 1999 Thankyou Music/Adm. by worshiptogether.com songs excl. UK & Europe, adm. by Kingsway Music. (tym@kingsway.co.uk). Used by permission.

169 The cross has said it all

Words and Music: Matt Redman and Martin Smith

1. The

cross has said it all,　　　the cross has said it all.
cross has said it all,　　　the cross has said it all.

I can't de-ny what you have shown,　the
I ne-ver re-cog-nised your touch, un-

© Copyright 1995 Thankyou Music/Adm. by worshiptogether.com songs excl. UK & Europe, adm. by Kingsway Music. (tym@kingsway.co.uk). Used by permission.

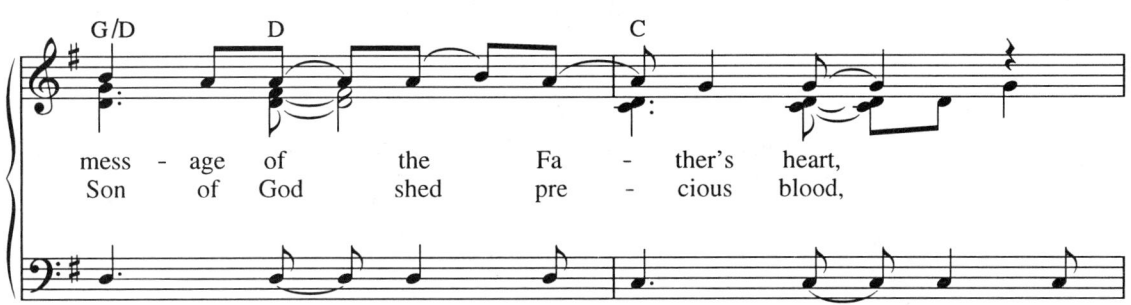

170 The crucible for silver

Words and Music: Martin Smith

1. The crucible for silver and the furnace for gold, but the Lord tests the heart of this child. Standing in all purity, God, our passion is for holiness, lead us to the secret place of praise.

© Copyright 1993 Thankyou Music/Adm. by worshiptogether.com songs excl. UK & Europe, adm. by Kingsway Music. (tym@kingsway.co.uk). Used by permission.

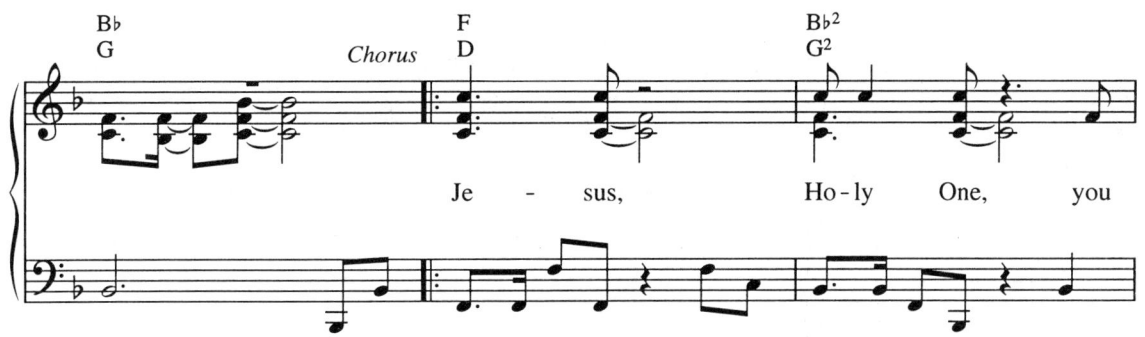
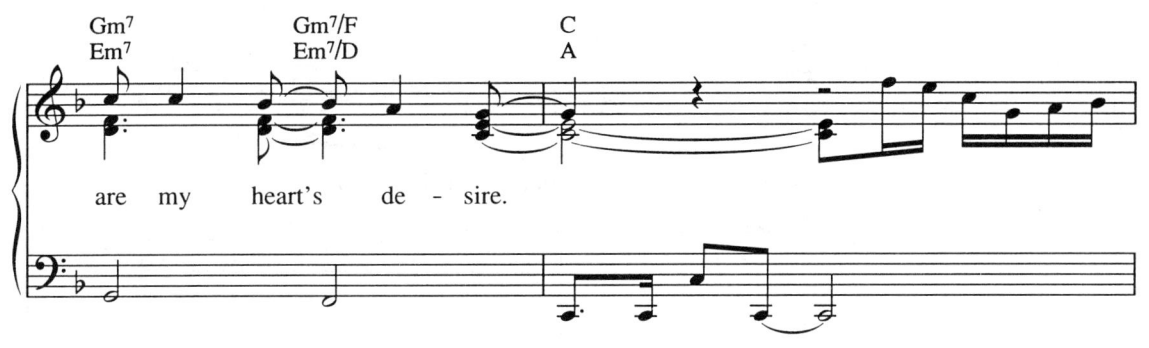
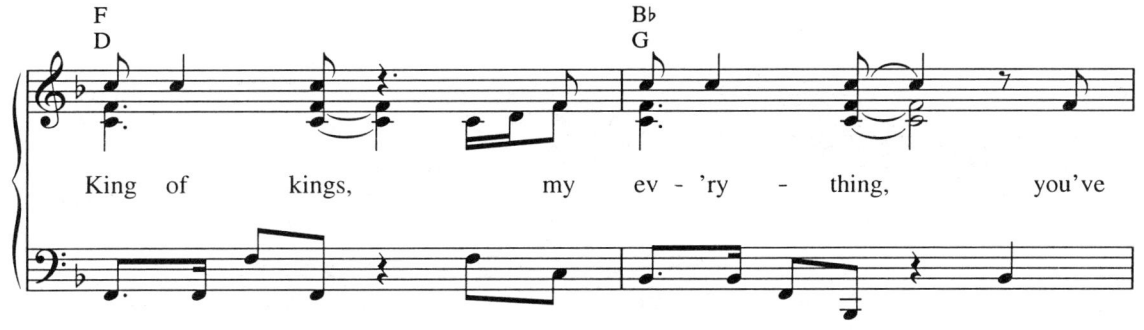
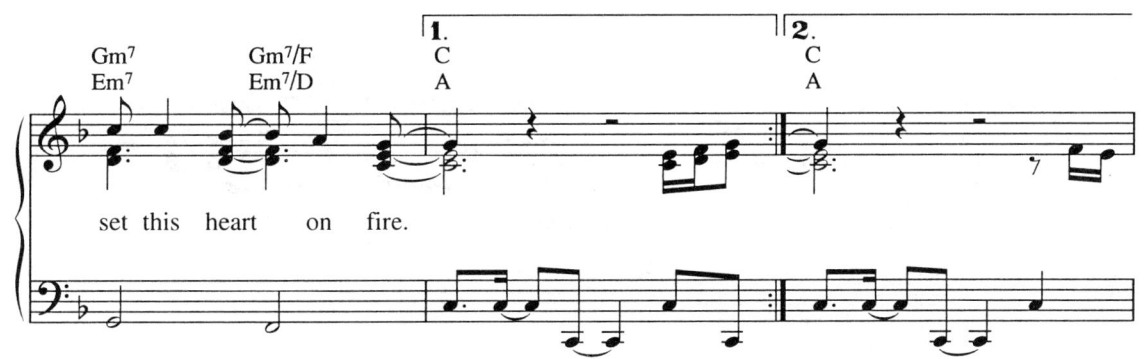

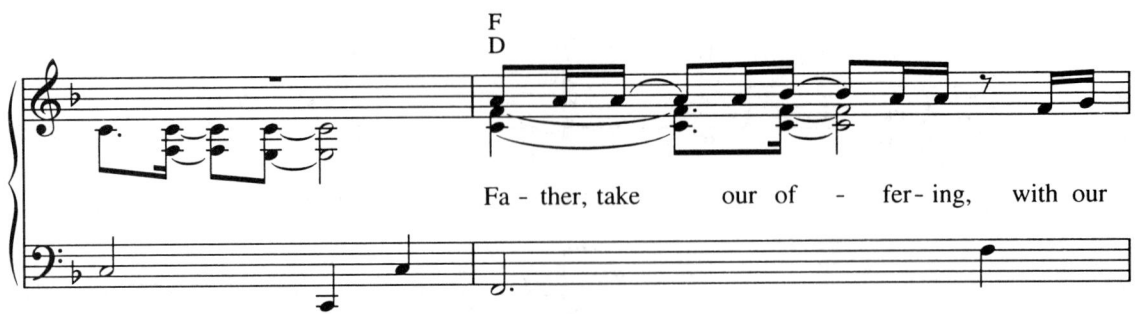
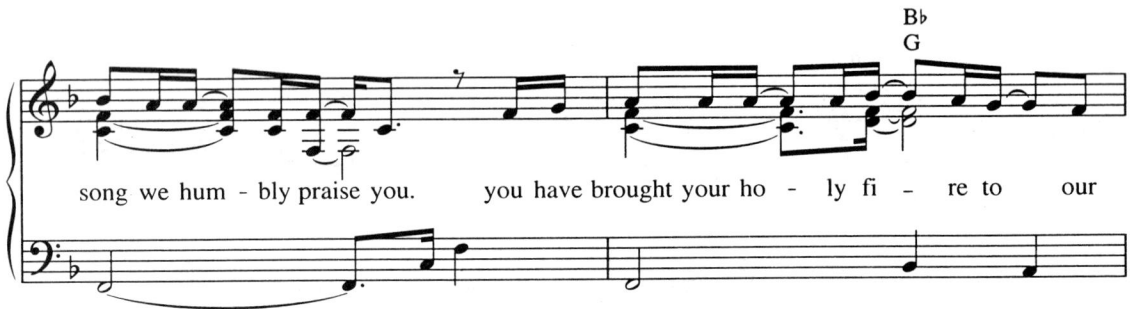

171 The King of love
The King has come
Words and Music: Stuart Townend and Kevin Jamieson

© Copyright 1997 Thankyou Music/Adm. by worshiptogether.com songs excl. UK & Europe, adm. by Kingsway Music. (tym@kingsway.co.uk). Used by permission.

2. My Lover's breath is sweetest wine,
   I am his prize, and he is mine;
   how can a sinner know such joy?
   because of Jesus.
   The wounds of love are in his hands,
   the price is paid for sinful man;
   accepted child, forgiven son:
   because of Jesus.

172 The Lord has led forth

Words and Music: Chris Bowater, adapted from Psalm 105: 43-45

© Copyright 1982 Sovereign Lifestyle Music, P.O. Box 356,
Leighton Buzzard, Beds., LU7 3WP, UK. Used by permission.

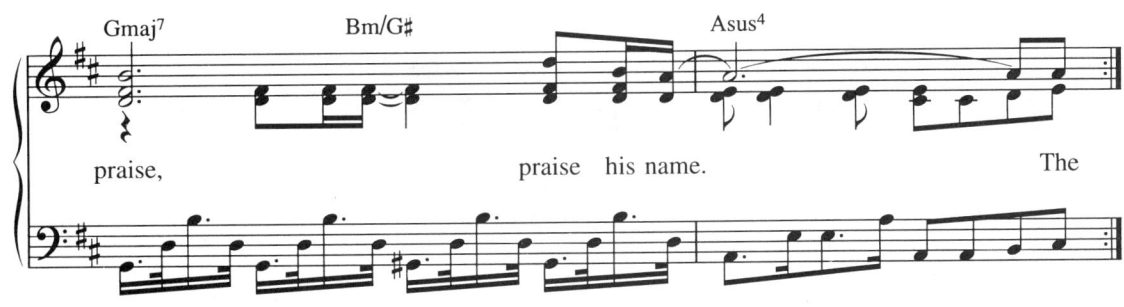

173 The Lord is present here

© Copyright 2001 Make Way Music, P.O. Box 263, Croydon, Surrey CR9 5AP, UK.
International copyright secured. All rights reserved. Used by permission.

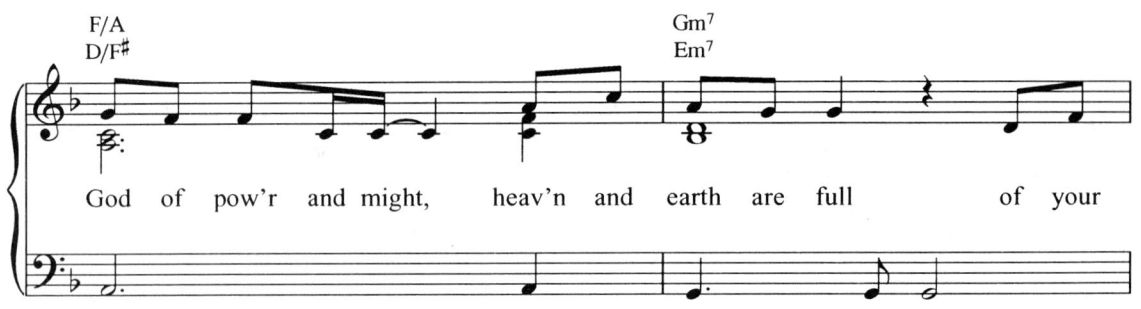

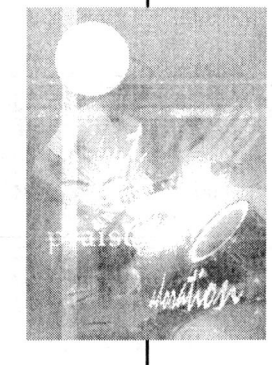

174 The price is paid

Words and Music: Graham Kendrick

2. The price is paid,
   see Satan flee away;
   for Jesus crucified
   destroys his pow'r.
   No more to pay,
   let accusation cease,
   in Christ there is
   no condemnation now.

3. The price is paid
   and by that scourging cruel
   he took our sicknesses
   as if his own.
   And by his wounds
   his body broken there,
   his healing touch
   may now by faith be known.

4. The price is paid,
   'Worthy the Lamb!' we cry,
   eternity shall never
   cease his praise.
   The church of Christ
   shall **rule** upon the earth,
   in Jesus' name
   we have authority.

175 There is a louder shout to come

Words and Music: Matt Redman

2. Now we see a part of this,
    one day we shall see in full;
    all the nations with one voice,
    all the people with one love.
    No one else will share your praise,
    nothing else can take your place;
    all the nations with one voice,
    all the people with one Lord.
    And what a song we'll sing upon that day!

3. Even now upon the earth
    there's a glimpse of all to come;
    many people with one voice,
    harmony of many tongues.
    We will all confess your name,
    you will be our only praise;
    all the nations with one voice,
    all the people with one God.
    And what a song we'll sing upon that day!

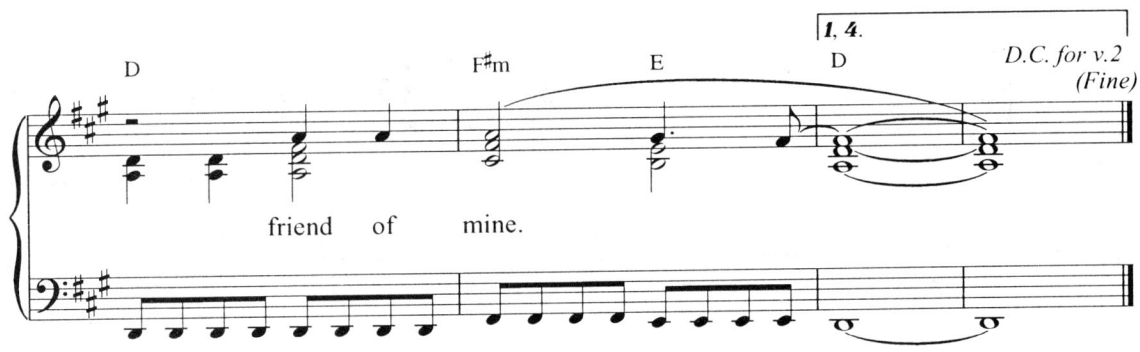

177 There is power in the name of Jesus

Words and Music: Noel Richards

© Copyright 1989 Thankyou Music/Adm. by worshiptogether.com songs excl. UK & Europe, adm. by Kingsway Music. (tym@kingsway.co.uk). Used by permission.

2. There is pow'r in the name of Jesus,
   like a sword in our hands.
   We declare in the name of Jesus
   we shall stand! We shall stand!
   At his name God's enemies
   shall be crushed beneath our feet,
   for there is no other name that is higher
   than Jesus!

178 There's a pageant of triumph in glory
Let God arise

Words and Music: David Fellingham

© Copyright 1999 Thankyou Music/Adm. by worshiptogether.com songs excl. UK & Europe, adm. by Kingsway Music. (tym@kingsway.co.uk) Used by permission.

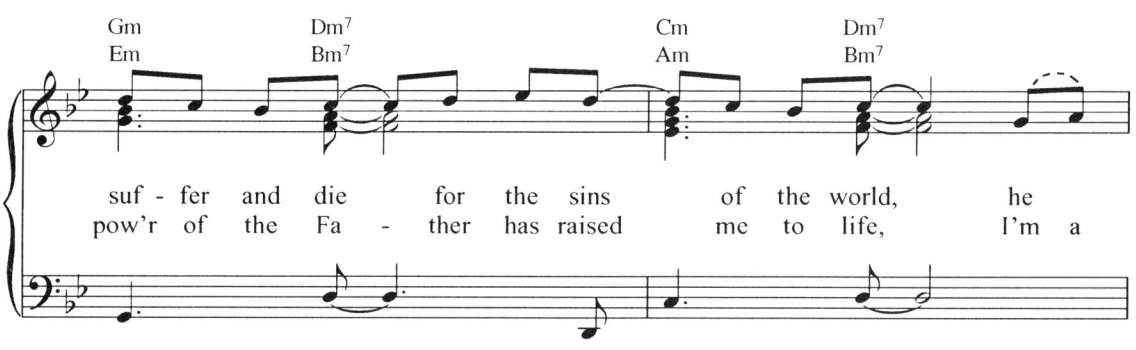

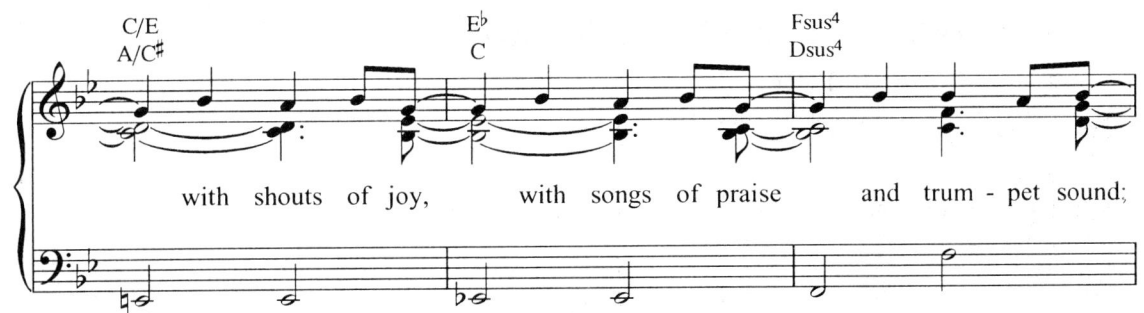

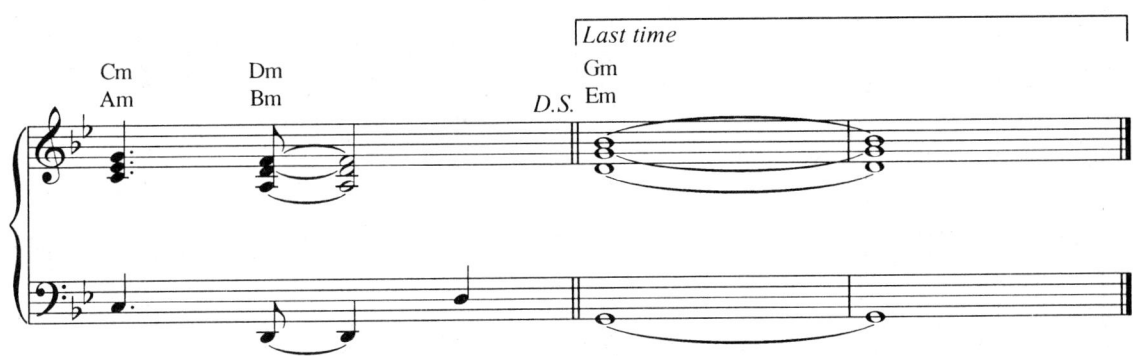

179 There's a place where the streets shine
Because of you
Words and Music: Paul Oakley

1. There's a place where the streets shine with the glory of the Lamb. There's a way, we can go there, we can live there beyond time. Because of you,

pain, no more sadness, no more suff'ring, no more tears. No more sin, no more sickness, no in- justice, no more

joy everlasting, there is gladness, there is peace. There is wine ever- flowing, there's a wedding, there's a

© Copyright 1995 Thankyou Music/Adm. by worshiptogether.com songs excl. UK & Europe, adm. by Kingsway Music. (tym@kingsway.co.uk). Used by permission.

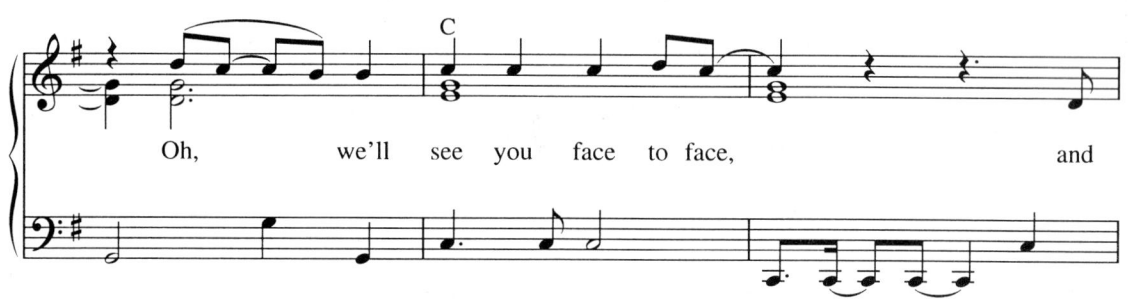

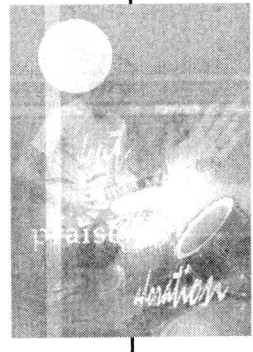

180 These are the days
Days of Elijah

Words and Music: Robin Mark

© Copyright 1996 Daybreak Music Ltd., PO Box 2848, Eastbourne, East Sussex BN20 7XP, UK.
All rights reserved. (info@daybreakmusic.co.uk). International copyright secured. Used by permission.

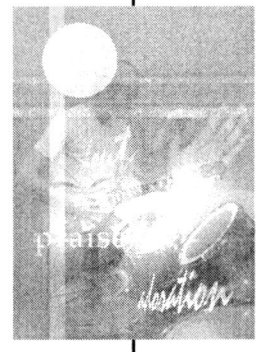

181 The Spirit lives to set us free
Walk in the light

Words: Damian Lundy

Music: Unknown
arr. Christopher Tambling

2. Jesus promised life to all,
   walk, walk in the light.
   The dead were wakened by his call,
   walk, walk in the light.

3. He died in pain on Calvary,
   walk, walk in the light,
   to save the lost like you and me,
   walk, walk in the light.

4. We know his death was not the end,
   walk, walk in the light.
   He gave his Spirit to be our friend,
   walk, walk in the light.

5. By Jesus' love our wounds are healed,
   walk, walk in the light.
   The Father's kindness is revealed,
   walk, walk in the light.

6. The Spirit lives in you and me,
   walk, walk in the light.
   His light will shine for all to see,
   walk, walk in the light.

Text and this arrangement © Copyright 1978, 1993 Kevin Mayhew Ltd.

182 The Spirit of the Lord

Words and Music: Graham Kendrick

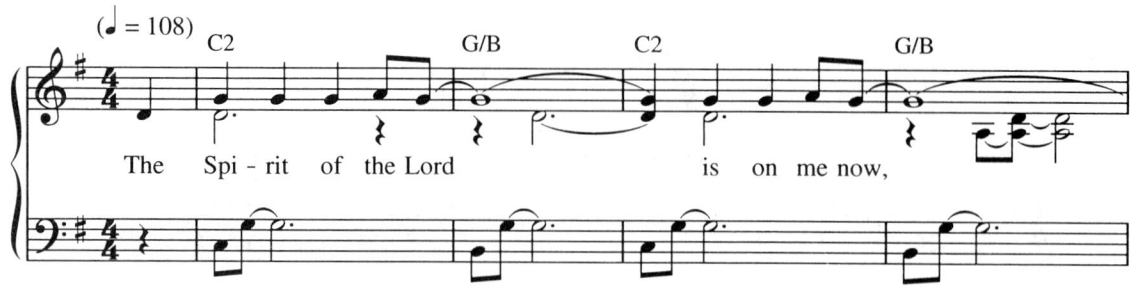

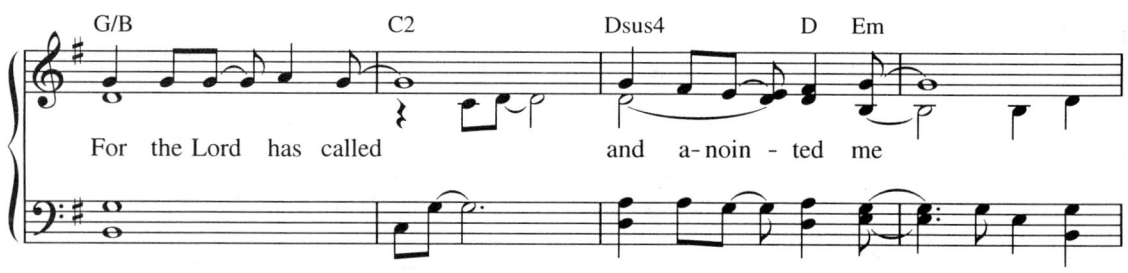

© 1997 Make Way Music, P.O. Box 264, Croydon, Surrey, CR9 5AP, UK.
International copyright secured. All rights reserved. Used by permission.

183 This Child

Words and Music: Graham Kendrick

© Copyright 1988 Make Way Music, P.O. Box 263, Croydon, Surrey,
CR9 5AP, UK. International copyright secured. All rights reserved. Used by permission.

2. This Child, rising on us like the sun,
   O this Child, given to light everyone,
   O this Child, guiding our feet on the pathway
   to peace on earth.

3. This Child, raising the humble and poor,
   O this Child, making the proud ones to fall;
   O this Child, filling the hungry with good things,
   this heavenly Child.

184 This is the air I breathe
Breathe

Words and Music: Marie Barnett
arr. Chris Mitchell

This is the air I breathe,
This is my dai - ly bread,

this is the air I breathe;
this is my dai - ly bread;

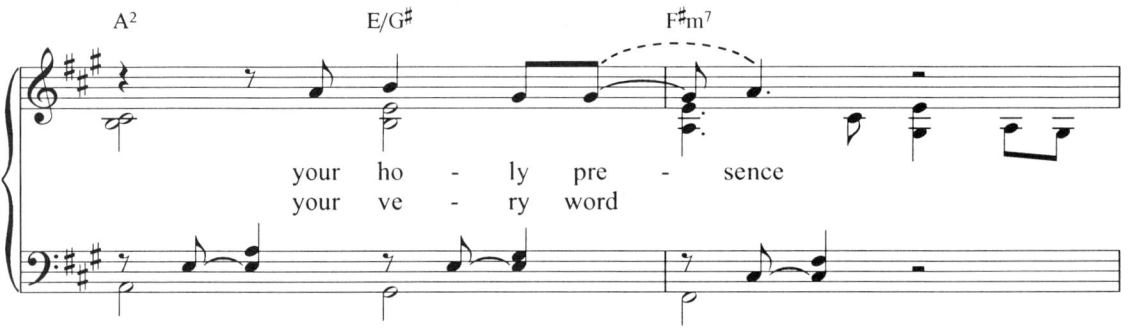

your ho - ly pre - sence
your ve - ry word

liv - ing in me.
spo - ken to me. And I,

© Copyright 1995 Mercy/Vineyard Publishing. Administered by CopyCare,
P.O. Box 77, Hailsham, East Sussex BN27 3EF, UK. (music@copycare.com). Used by permission.

185 This is the best place
Worshipping the living God

Words and Music: Ian White

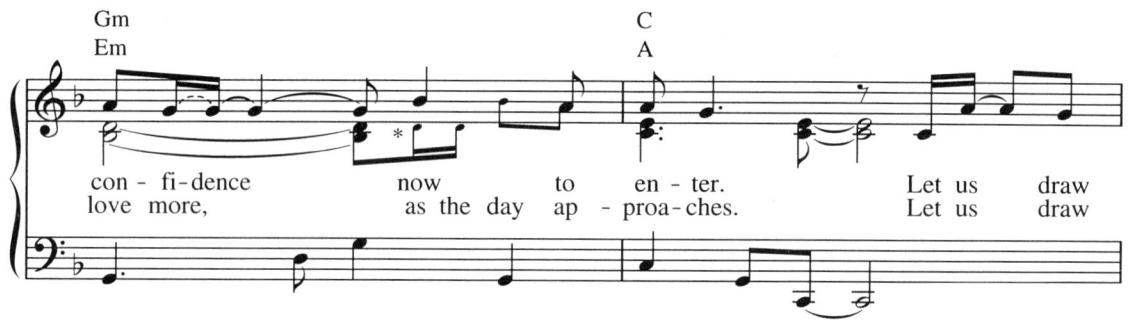
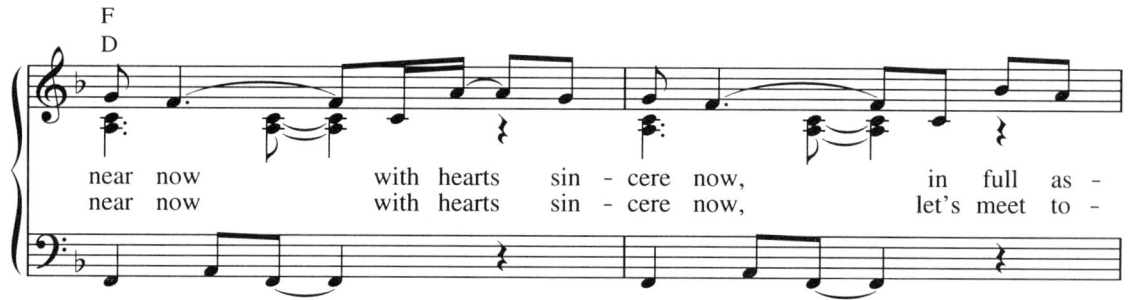
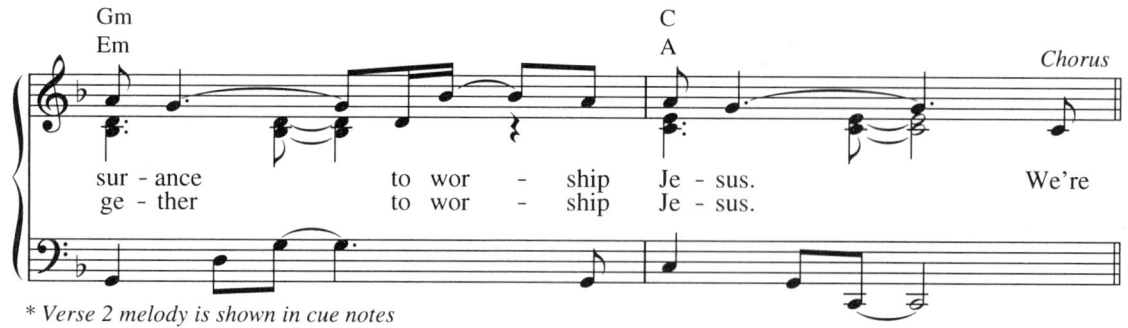

* Verse 2 melody is shown in cue notes

© 1997 Thankyou Music/Adm. by worshiptogether.com songs excl. UK & Europe, adm. by Kingsway Music. (tym@kingsway.co.uk). Worldwide excluding Australasia. Used by permission.

187 This is the time
Distant thunder
Words and Music: David Palmer

© 1997 David Palmer (dipalmeroz@yahoo.co.uk). Used by permission.

189 To be in your presence
My desire

Words and Music: Noel Richards

2. To rest in your presence, not rushing away,
   to cherish each moment, here I would stay.

© Copyright 1991 Thankyou Music/Adm. by worshiptogether.com songs excl. UK & Europe, adm. by Kingsway Music. (tym@kingsway.co.uk). Used by permission.

190 To him who loves us

Words and Music: Bryn Haworth

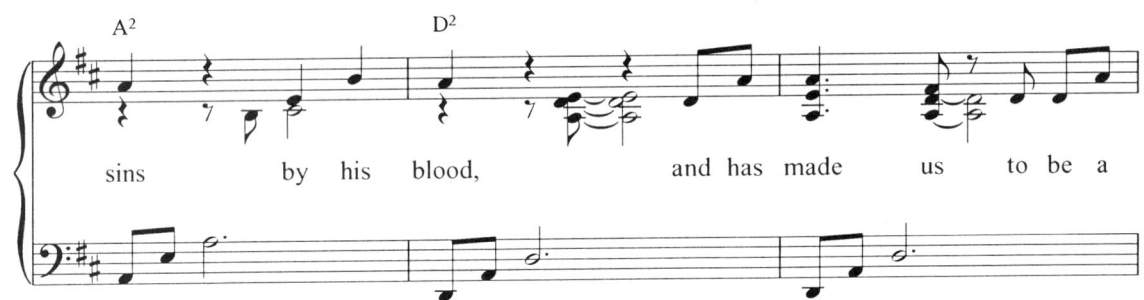

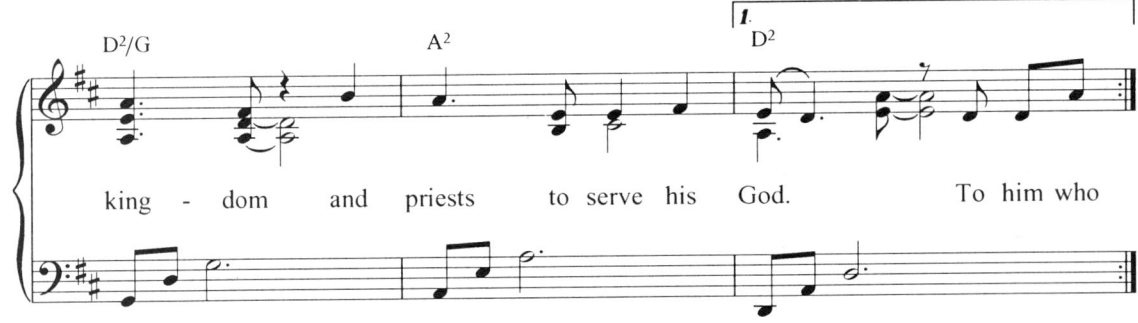

© Copyright 1996 Thankyou Music/Adm. by worshiptogether.com songs excl. UK & Europe, adm. by Kingsway Music. (tym@kingsway.co.uk). Used by permission.

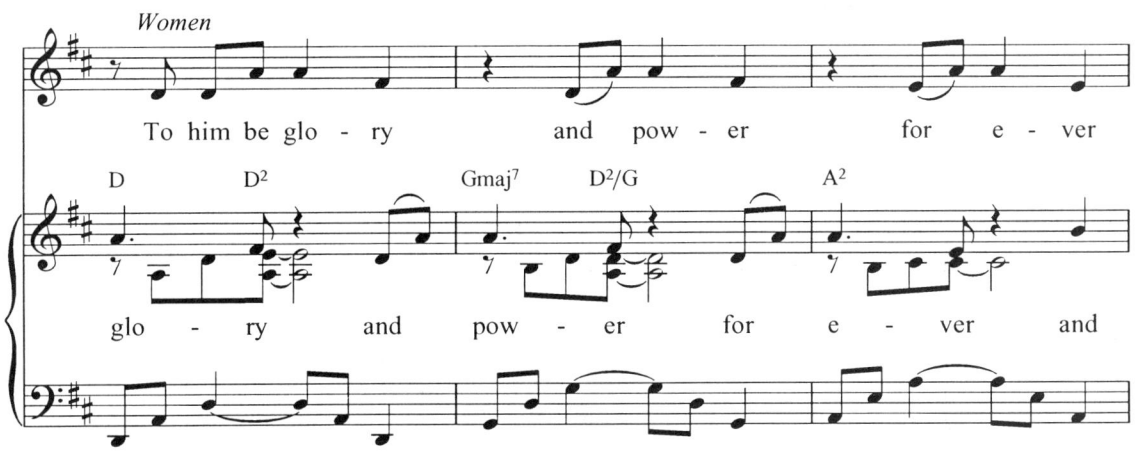

191 To the King eternal

Words and Music: Graham Kendrick

© Copyright 1999 Ascent Music, P.O. Box 263, Croydon, Surrey CR9 5AP, UK.
International copyright secured. All rights reserved. Used by permission.

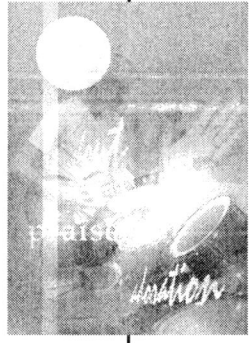

192 To you, O Lord, I lift up my soul

Words and Music: Graham Kendrick

1. To you, O Lord, I lift up my soul.
   In you I trust, O my God.
   Do not let me be put to shame,
   nor let my enemies triumph over me.

2. Show me your ways and teach me your paths.
   Guide me in truth, lead me on;
   for you're my God, you are my Saviour.
   My hope is in you each moment of the day.

Chorus
No one whose hope is in you

© Copyright 1997 Make Way Music, P.O. Box 263, Croydon, Surrey, CR9 5AP, UK.
International copyright secured. All rights reserved. Used by permission.

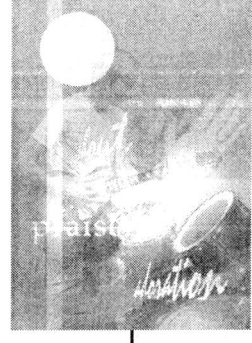

193 Trust in the Lord

Words and Music: Paul Critchley

© Copyright 1999 Kevin Mayhew Ltd.

194 We ask you, O Lord
The latter rain
Words and Music: Richard Lewis

Prayerfully, with strength

We ask you, O Lord, for the rain of your

Spirit. We ask you, O Lord, for the rain of your

Spirit, for now is the time, for

now is the time of the latter rain,

© Copyright 1994 Thankyou Music/Adm. by worshiptogether.com songs excl. UK & Europe, adm. by Kingsway Music. (tym@kingsway.co.uk). Used by permission.

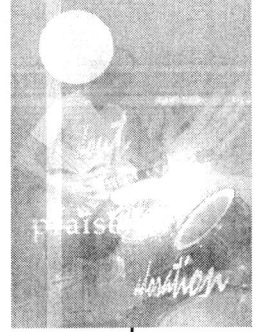

195 We believe

Words and Music: Graham Kendrick

© Copyright 1986 Thankyou Music/Adm. by worshiptogether.com songs excl. UK & Europe, adm. by Kingsway Music. (tym@kingsway.co.uk). Used by permission.

2. We believe he sends his Spirit
   on his church with gifts of pow'r.
   God, his word of truth affirming,
   sends us to the nations now.
   He will come again in glory,
   judge the living and the dead.
   Ev'ry knee shall bow before him,
   then must ev'ry tongue confess.

196 We bow down

Words and Music: Viola Grafstom

© Copyright 1996 Thankyou Music/Adm. by worshiptogether.com songs excl. UK & Europe, adm. by Kingsway Music. (tym@kingsway.co.uk). Used by permission.

197 We have come to a holy mountain
Holy mountain

Words and Music: Russ Hughes
arr. Richard Lewis

(♩ = 94)

1. We have come to a holy mountain,
joining angels in celebration,
a thousand thousand lift their voices
as the first-born Church sings her praises
to the Holy One, to the Holy One.

© Copyright 2000 Joshua Music/Alliance Media Ltd., Administered by CopyCare,
P.O. Box 77, Hailsham, East Sussex BN27 3EF, UK. (music@copycare.com). Used by permission.

198 We have sung our songs of victory
How long?

Words and Music: Stuart Townend

2. Lord, we know your heart is broken
   by the evil that you see,
   and you've stayed your hand of judgement
   for you plan to set men free.
   But the land is still in darkness,
   and we've fled from what is right;
   we have failed the silent children
   who will never see the light.

3. But I know a day is coming
   when the deaf will hear his voice,
   when the blind will see their Saviour,
   and the lame will leap for joy.
   When the widow finds a husband
   who will always love his bride,
   and the orphan finds a father
   who will never leave her side.

(Final Chorus)
How long before your glory lights the skies?
How long before your radiance lifts our eyes?
How long before your fragrance fills the air?
How long before the earth resounds with songs of joy?

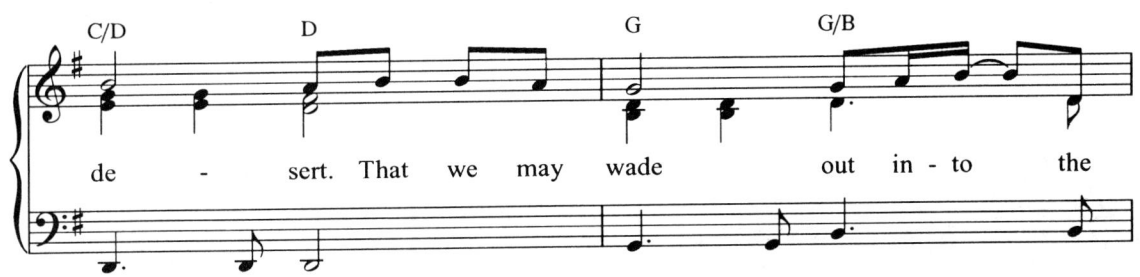

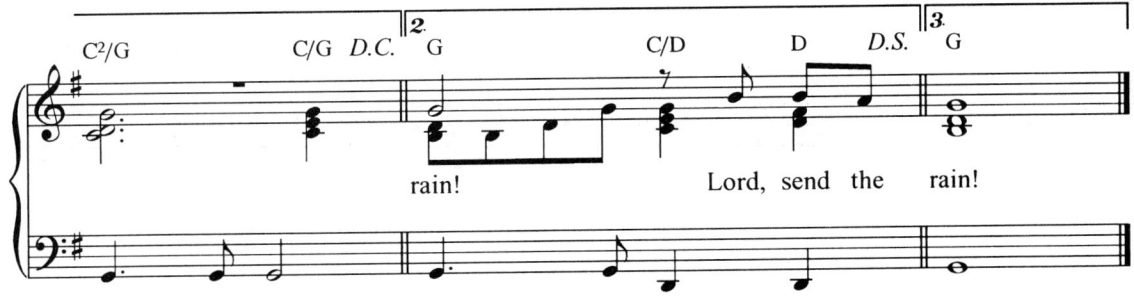

2. Move through our land,
   give to each one the power of your Spirit.
   Heal broken lives,
   sweep sin aside, come rain down on ev'ry life.
   That all may know that Jesus reigns,
   that all may see you in your sov'reign pow'r,
   send your Holy Spirit.

200 Welcome, King of kings

Words and Music: Noel Richards

© Copyright 1991 Thankyou Music/Adm. by worshiptogether.com songs excl. UK & Europe, adm. by Kingsway Music. (tym@kingsway.co.uk). Used by permission.

2. Let all creation bow down
   at the sound of your name.
   Let ev'ry tongue now confess,
   the Lord God reigns.

201 Well, I hear they're singing in the streets
I've found Jesus

Words and Music: Martin Smith arr. L. Hills

© Copyright 1994 Curious? Music UK. PO Box 40, Arundel, West Sussex BN18 0UQ, UK.
Used by permission.

203 We want to see Jesus lifted high

Words and Music: Doug Horley

© Copyright 1993 Thankyou Music/Adm. by worshiptogether.com songs excl. UK & Europe, adm. by Kingsway Music. (tym@kingsway.co.uk). Used by permission.

204 What a friend I've found
Jesus, friend for ever

Words and Music: Martin Smith

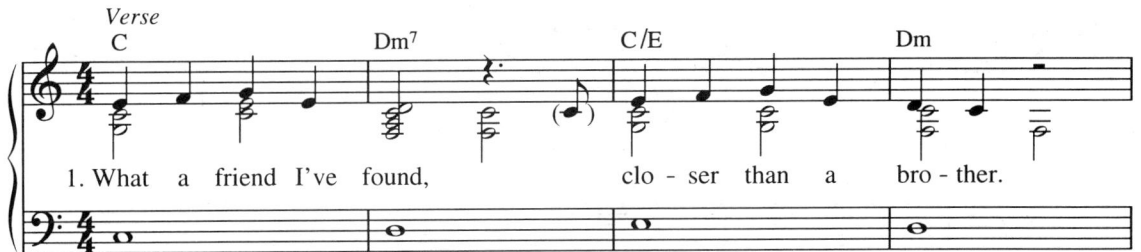

2. What a hope I've found,
   more faithful than a mother.
   It would break my heart,
   to ever lose each other.

© Copyright 1996 Curious? Music UK. PO Box 40, Arundel, West Sussex BN18 0UQ, UK.
Used by permission.

205 What kind of love is this

Words and Music: Bryn and Sally Haworth

1. What kind of love is this that

gave it-self for me? I

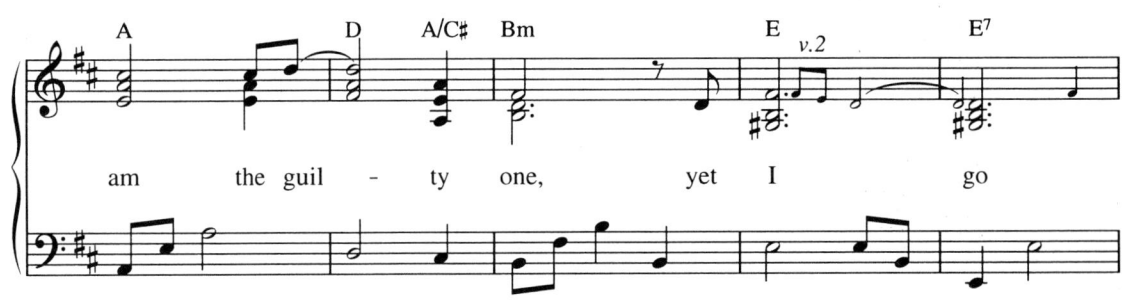

am the guil-ty one, yet I go

free. What kind of love is this,

© Copyright 1983 Signalgrade/Kingsway Music. (tym@kingsway.co.uk). Worldwide.
Used by permission.

2. What kind of man is this
   that died in agony?
   He who had done no wrong
   was crucified for me.
   What kind of man is this
   who laid aside his throne,
   that I may know the love of God?
   What kind of man is this?

3. By grace I have been saved;
   it is the gift of God.
   He destined me to be his child,
   such is his love.
   No eye has ever seen,
   no ear has ever heard,
   nor has the heart of man conceived
   what kind of love is this.

206 What love is this?
I surrender

Words and Music: Dave Bilbrough

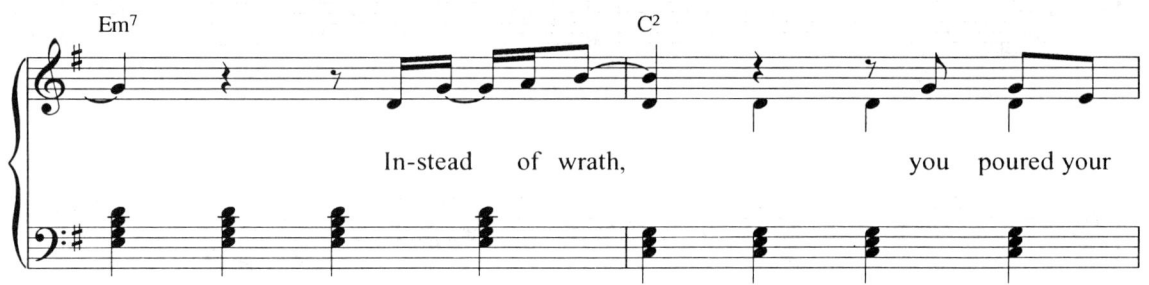

© Copyright 1999 Thankyou Music/Adm. by worshiptogether.com songs excl. UK & Europe, adm. by Kingsway Music. (tym@kingsway.co.uk). Used by permission.

2. What love is this
   that comes to save?
   Upon the cross
   you bore my guilt and shame.
   To you alone
   I give my heart
   and worship you.

3. A greater love
   no man has seen;
   it breaks sin's pow'r
   and sets this pris'ner free.
   With all I have
   and all I am,
   I worship you.

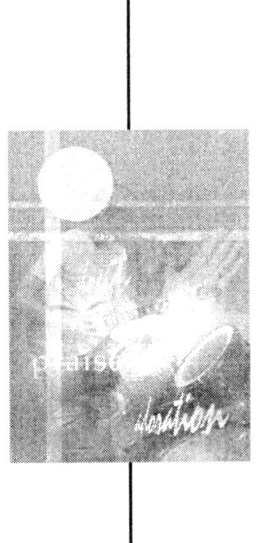

207 What wondrous love is this
Upon a cross of shame

Words and Music: James Wright
arr. Richard Lewis

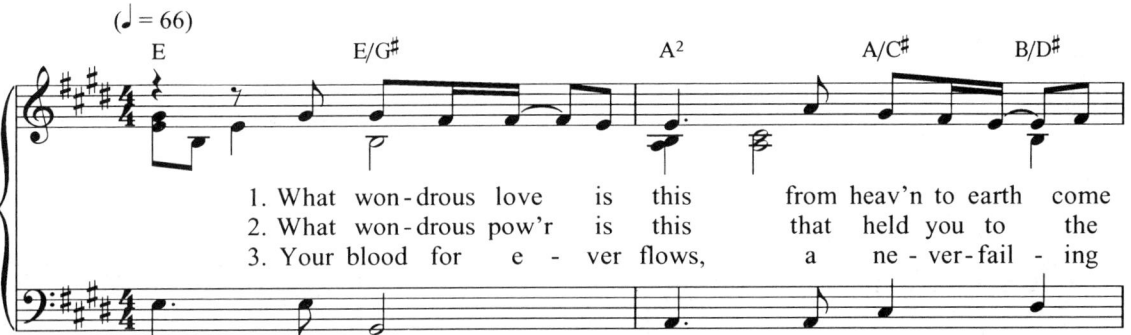

1. What won-drous love is this from heav'n to earth come
2. What won-drous pow'r is this that held you to the
3. Your blood for e - ver flows, a ne-ver-fail-ing

down, the great-est gift of all was giv - en.
cross, not the a - go - ny of thorns and nails,
stream of for-give - ness, of pow'r and cleans - ing.

The ho - ly Lamb of God was lift - ed up to
but e - ver-last - ing love and waves of ho - ly
And your cross for e - ver stands from age to age the

die that we might have life.

© Copyright 2001 Kevin Mayhew Ltd.

208 When I pray
Fire fall

Words and Music: Richard Lewis

© Copyright 2001 Kevin Mayhew Ltd.

2. For my praise, it burns like incense,
   and my prayers rise to your throne;
   they release fire from the altar,
   and the Devil cannot stand,
   and the Devil cannot stand,
   and the Devil cannot stand when I pray.

209 When I sing my praise
When I worship you

Words and Music: Noel Richards and Tricia Richards

1. When I sing my praise to you, I am lifted up to
2. Heaven is where I belong, where the angels sing be-

higher ground. Something happens in my soul when I
fore your throne. I am caught up in their sound, when I

lift my voice to worship you. Feels like sunshine on
lift my voice to worship you. From beyond where eyes

© Copyright 1999 Thankyou Music/Adm. by worshiptogether.com songs excl. UK & Europe, adm. by Kingsway Music. (tym@kingsway.co.uk). Used by permission.

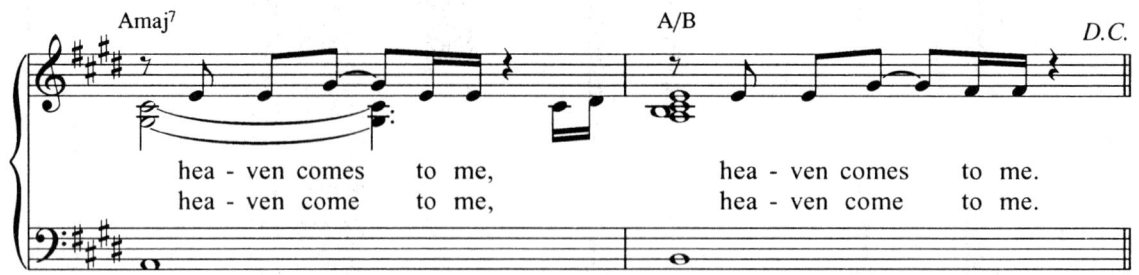

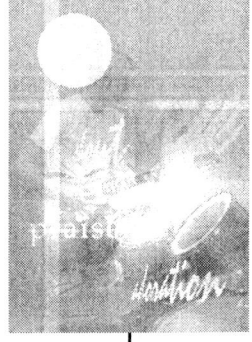

210 When the music fades
The heart of worship
Words and Music: Matt Redman

© Copyright 1997 Thankyou Music/Adm. by worshiptogether.com songs excl. UK & Europe, adm. by Kingsway Music. (tym@kingsway.co.uk). Used by permission.

211 Who can sound the depths of sorrow

Words and Music: Graham Kendrick

© Copyright 1988 Make Way Music, P.O. Box 263, Croydon, Surrey, CR9 5AP, UK.
International copyright secured. All rights reserved. Used by permission.

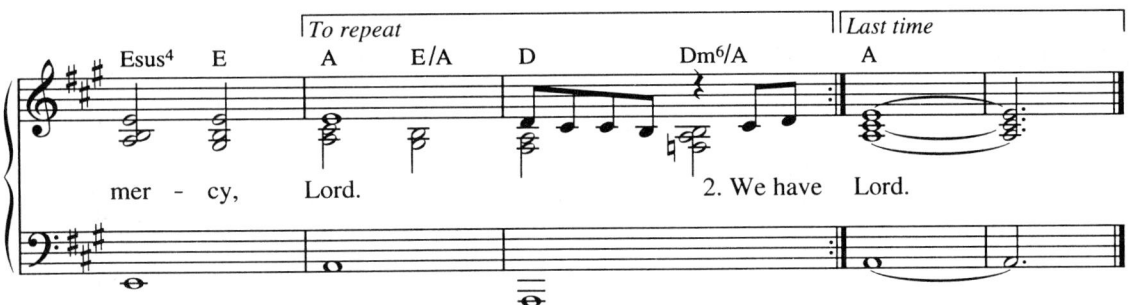

2. We have scorned the truth you gave us,
   we have bowed to other lords.
   We have sacrificed the children
   on the altar of our gods.
   O let truth again shine on us,
   let your holy fear descend:
   upon our nation, upon our nation
   have mercy, Lord.

   (Men)
3. Who can stand before your anger?
   Who can face your piercing eyes?
   For you love the weak and helpless,
   and you hear the victims' cries.
   (All)
   Yes, you are a God of justice,
   and your judgement surely comes:
   upon our nation, upon our nation
   have mercy, Lord.

   (Women)
4. Who will stand against the violence?
   Who will comfort those who mourn?
   In an age of cruel rejection,
   who will build for love a home?
   (All)
   Come and shake us into action,
   come and melt our hearts of stone:
   upon your people, upon your people
   have mercy, Lord.

5. Who can sound the depths of mercy
   in the Father heart of God?
   For there is a Man of sorrows
   who for sinners shed his blood.
   He can heal the wounds of nations,
   he can wash the guilty clean:
   because of Jesus, because of Jesus
   have mercy, Lord.

Note: some congregations may wish to add to the effectiveness of this song by transposing the final verse up a semitone, into B♭ major.

212 Who is there like you?

Words and Music: Paul Oakley

213 Who paints the skies?
River of fire
Words and Music: Stuart Townend

© Copyright 1995 Thankyou Music/Adm. by worshiptogether.com songs excl. UK & Europe, adm. by Kingsway Music. (tym@kingsway.co.uk) Used by permission.

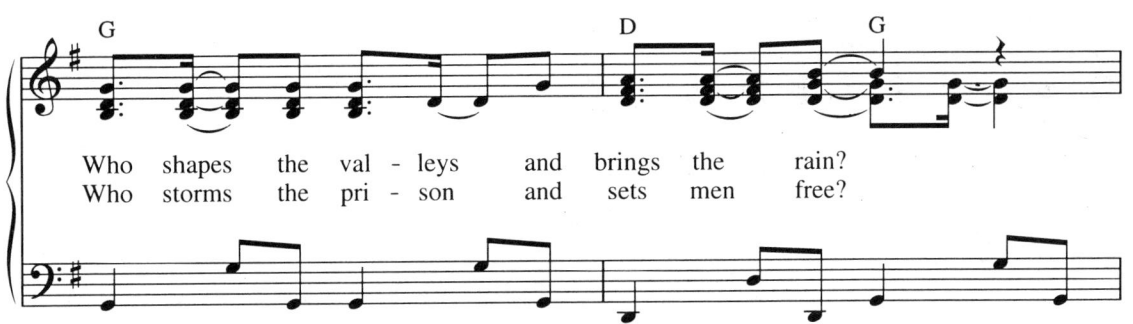

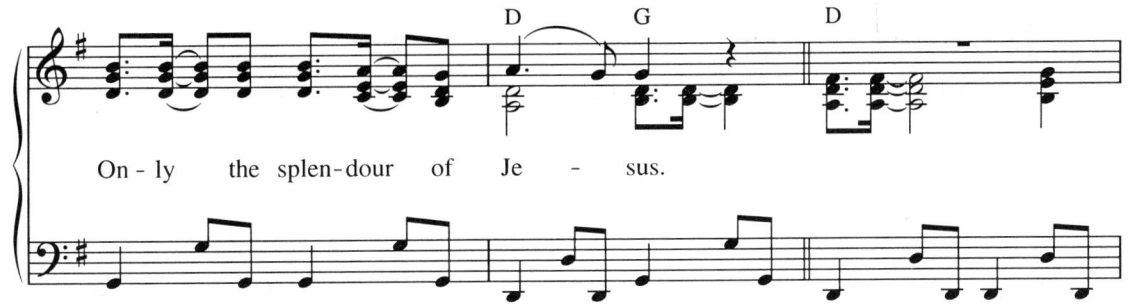

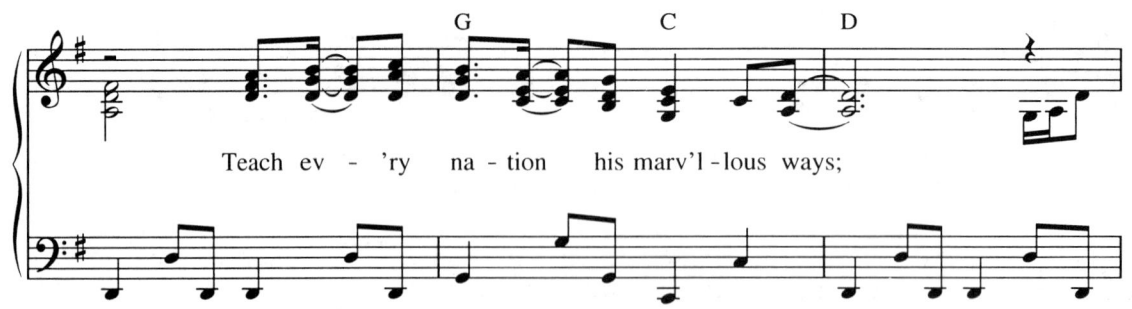

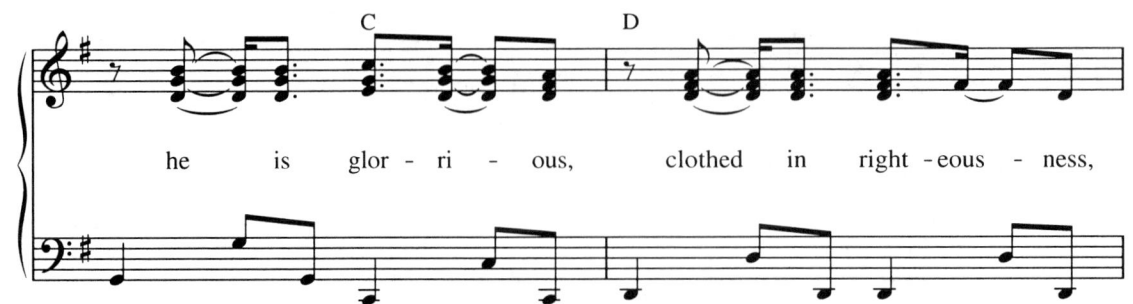

214 Who sees it all

Words and Music: Graham Kendrick

3. Who knows the fears that drive a choice,
   unburies pain and gives it voice?
   And who can wash a memory,
   or take the sting of death away?

4. Whose anger burns at what we've done,
   then bears our sin as if his own?
   Who will receive us as we are,
   whose arms are wide and waiting now?

5. Whose broken heart upon a cross
   won freedom, joy and peace for us?
   Whose blood redeems, who ever lives
   and all because of love forgives?

215 With all my heart

Words and Music: Steve McGregor

Steve McGregor © Copyright 1995 Remission Music UK/Sovereign Lifestyle Music.
P.O. Box 356, Leighton Buzzard LU7 3PW, UK.

2. Nothing compares to your faithfulness,
   no greater love in earth or above:
   so I'll declare, my heart is safe in your arms.

216 Wonderful grace

Words and Music: John Pantry

1. Wonderful grace, that gives what I don't deserve, pays me what Christ has earned, then lets me go free. Wonderful grace, that gives me the time to change, washes away the stains that once covered me. And

© Copyright 1990 HarperCollins Religious. Administered by CopyCare,
PO Box 77, Hailsham, East Sussex BN27 3EF, UK. (music@copycare.com). Used by permission.

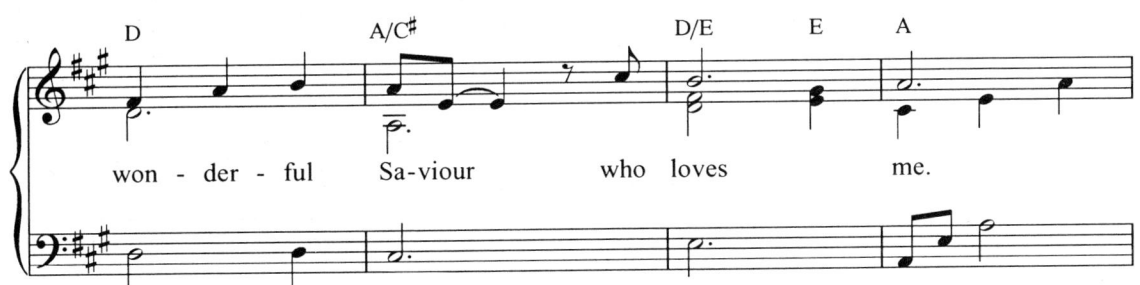

2. Wonderful grace, that held in the face of death,
   breathed in its latest breath forgiveness for me.
   Wonderful love, whose pow'r can break ev'ry chain,
   giving us life again, setting us free.

217 Worthy

Words and Music: David Wellington
arr. Richard Lewis

Wor-thy, wor-thy, wor-thy, wor-thy, Je-sus.

Last time Fine
To continue

And while I live, my tongue shall tell; and while I breathe, my heart shall sing; I will not wait for

© Copyright 2001 Kevin Mayhew Ltd.

218 You are merciful to me

Words and Music: Ian White

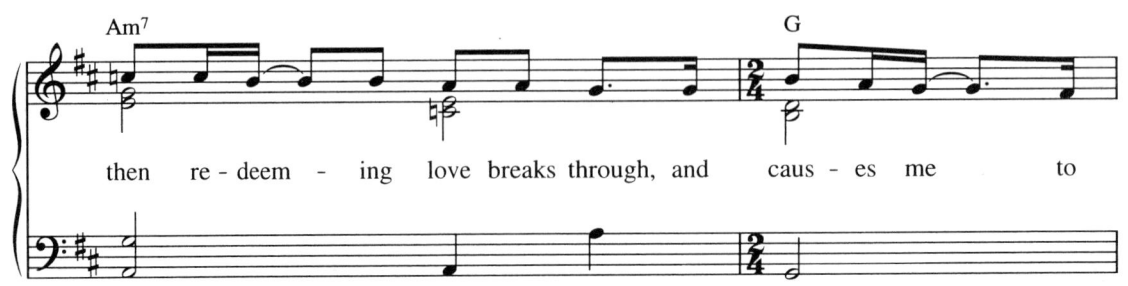

© Copyright 1997 Thankyou Music/Adm. by worshiptogether.com songs excl. UK & Europe, adm. by Kingsway Music. (tym@kingsway.co.uk). Worldwide excluding Australasia. Used by permission.

219 You are my anchor

Words and Music: Stuart Townend

1. You are my anchor, my light and my salvation. You are my refuge, my heart will not fear. Though my foes surround me on ev'ry hand, they will stumble and fall while in grace I stand. In my day

Lord, make straight the path before me. Do not forsake me, my hope is in you. As I walk through life, I am confident I will see your goodness with ev'ry step, and my heart

© Copyright 2001 Thankyou Music/Adm. by worshiptogether.com songs excl. UK & Europe,
adm. by Kingsway Music. (tym@kingsway.co.uk). Used by permission.

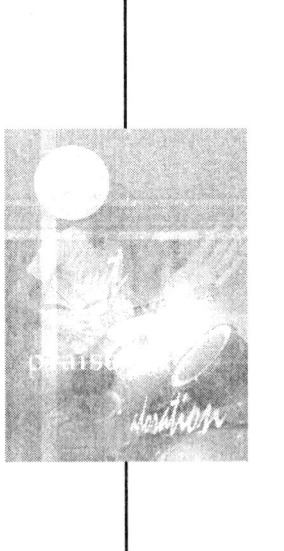

220 You came from heaven's splendour
Jesus, almighty Saviour

Words and Music: James Wright
arr. Richard Lewis

1. You came from heaven's splendour to earth's humanity, healing the broken-hearted, setting them free. But for the joy that followed you gave up ev'rything;

2. There in the tomb your broken body in silence lay, but for three days, three nights it did not see decay. You had a greater purpose, you had a greater plan

© Copyright 2001 Kevin Mayhew Ltd.

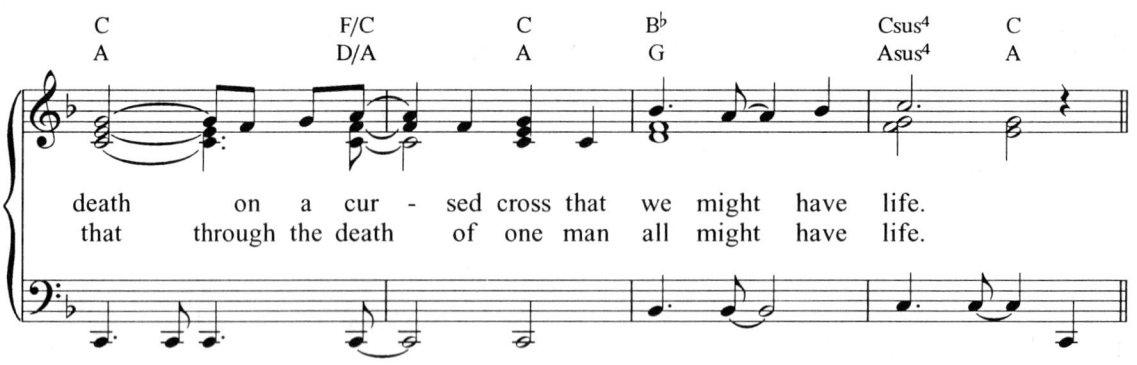
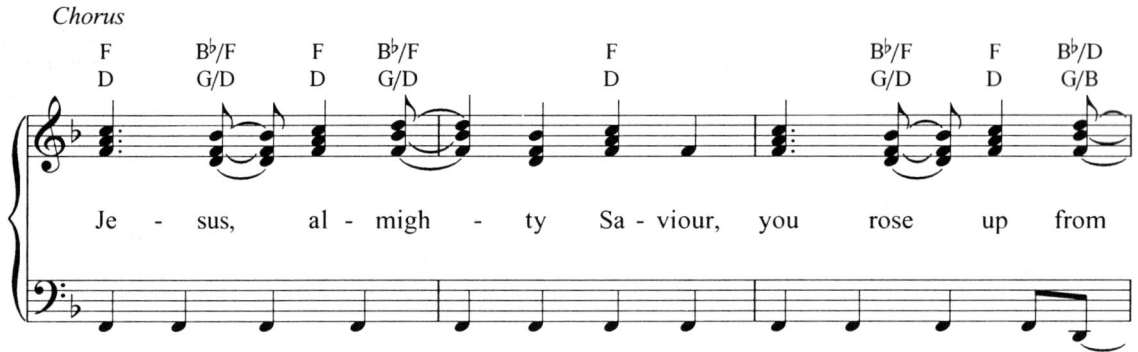

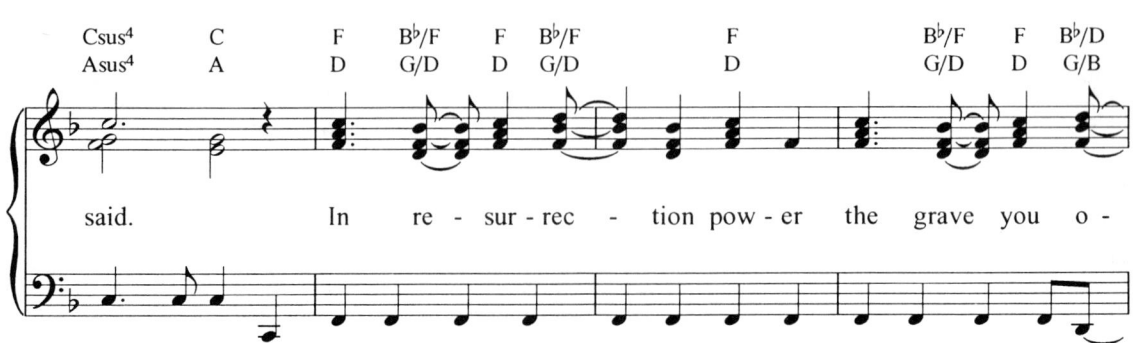

221 You laid aside your majesty
I really want to worship you, my Lord
Words and Music: Noel Richards

© Copyright 1985 Thankyou Music/Adm. by worshiptogether.com songs excl. UK & Europe, adm. by Kingsway Music. (tym@kingsway.co.uk). Used by permission.

222 You laid down your majesty
That's why I give my life

Words and Music: James Wright
arr. Richard Lewis

1. You laid down your majesty to show us your love
love is a mys-te-ry to lay down your life

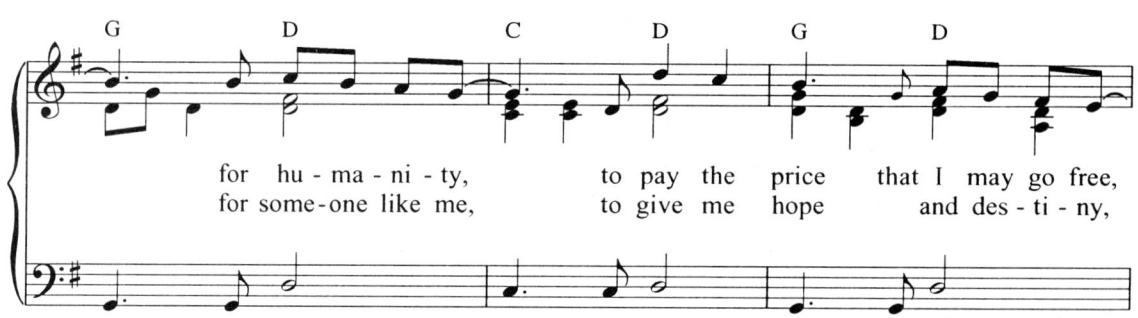

for hu-ma-ni-ty, to pay the price that I may go free,
for some-one like me, to give me hope and des-ti-ny,

O Lamb of God, my sac-ri-fice. And then you
O Lamb of God, my sac-ri-fice. Now I have

rose up-on the third day con-quer-ing death,
peace deep in my heart, the kind that this world

© Copyright 2001 Kevin Mayhew Ltd.

223 Your love
Pour over me

Words and Music: Stuart Townend

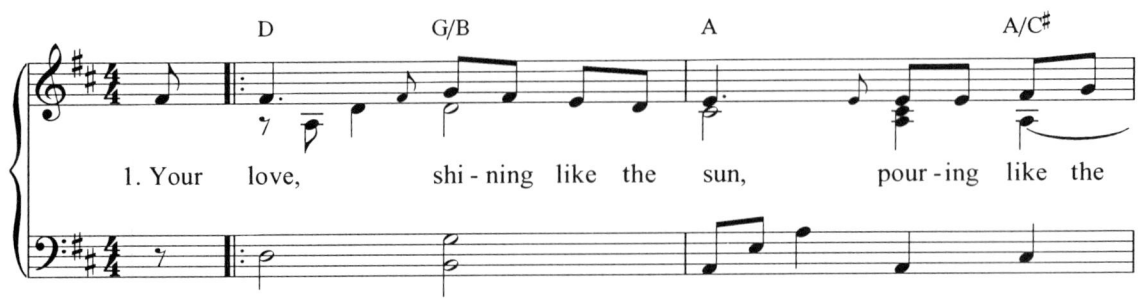

© 1999 Thankyou Music/Adm. by worshiptogether.com songs excl. UK & Europe, adm. by Kingsway Music. (tym@kingsway.co.uk). Used by permission.

2. Your grace frees me from the past,
   it purges every sin,
   it purifies my heart
   and heals me from within,
   I receive your grace.

3. I come and lay my burden down
   gladly at your feet.
   I'm op'ning up my heart,
   come make this joy complete,
   I receive your grace.

224 Your mercy flows

Words and Music: Wes Sutton

© Copyright 1987 Sovereign Lifestyle Music Ltd, P.O. Box 356,
Leighton Buzzard, Bedfordshire, LU7 3WP, UK. Used by permission.

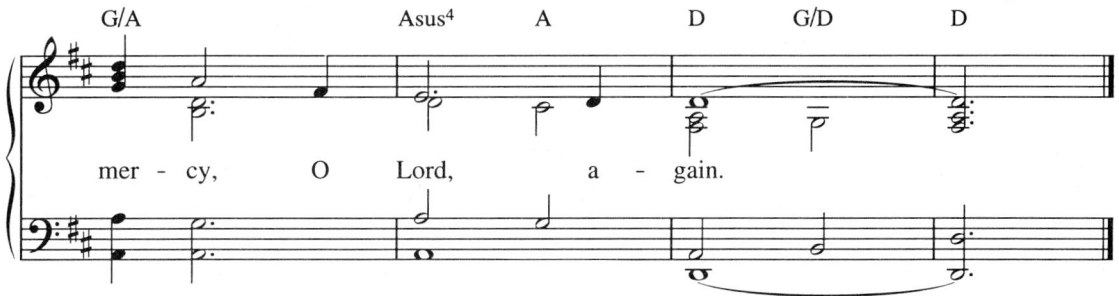

2. Your church once great, though standing clothed in sorrow,
   is even still the bride that you adore;
   revive your church, that we again may honour
   our God and King, our Master and our Lord.

3. As we have slept, this nation has been taken
   by ev'ry sin we have ever known,
   so at its gates, though burnt by fire and broken,
   in Jesus' name we come to take our stand.

225 Your name is great

Words and Music: Trish Morgan

© Copyright 1997 Radical UK Music/Sovereign Music UK, PO Box 356,
Leighton Buzzard, LU7 3WP, UK. Used by permission.

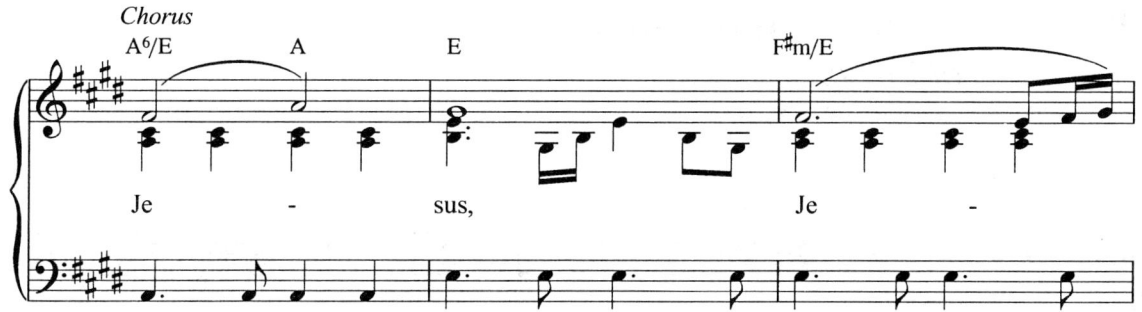

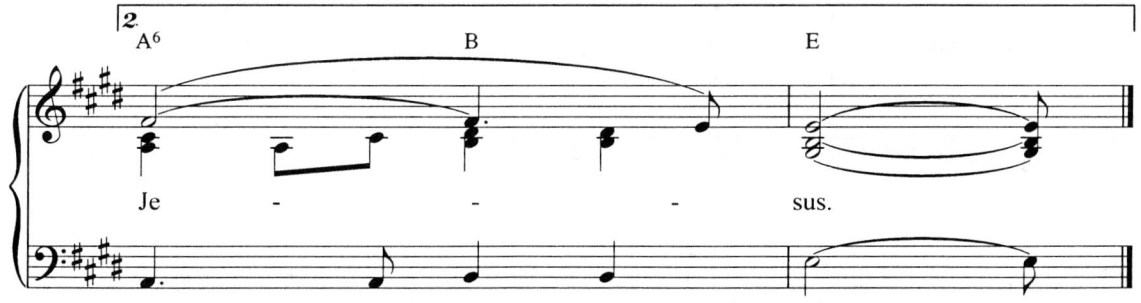

2. Your name is strong,
   your name is true;
   Lord, no one else can love like you.
   Your name can save,
   the waters part;
   your name can heal the broken heart.

3. Your name breaks chains.
   your pow'r is shown;
   over foreign skies your name is known.
   Your name brings light,
   the demons flee;
   your name will last eternally.

226 You're the Lion of Judah
Lion of Judah
Words and Music: Robin Mark

1. You're the Lion of Judah, the Lamb that was slain, you ascended to heaven and evermore will reign; at the end of the age when the earth you reclaim, you will gather the nations before you. And the eyes of all men will be fixed on the Lamb who was crucified, for with wisdom and mercy and justice he

2. There's a shield in our hand and a sword at our side, there's a fire in our spirit that cannot be denied; as the Father has told us: for these you have died, for the nations that gather before you. And the ears of all men need to hear of the Lamb who was crucified, who descended to hell yet was raised up to

© Copyright 1996 Daybreak Music Ltd, PO Box 2848,
Eastbourne, BN20 7XP, UK. Used by permission.

Index

Index of Songwriters, Authors and Composers

Atkinson, Jennifer 86

Baker, Geoff 142
Baker, Marilyn 101
Banderet, Paul 102
Bankhead, Dave 27
Barnett, Marie 184
Baughen, Michael 71, 110
Bell, Stuart 66
Bilbrough, Dave 1, 3, 10, 16, 64, 144, 148, 166, 206
Bond, Derek 13
Bowater, Chris 28, 31, 45, 46, 52, 59, 69, 87, 95, 105, 153, 172, 186
Brown, Dougie 156
Bryant, Dave 96

Clifton, Dave 150
Coates, Gerald 47, 50
Cooper, Jarrod 48, 103
Critchley, Paul 193
Crocker, Elisabeth 71
Cruikshank, Paul 66

Doerksen, Brian 26
Dudley-Smith, Timothy 71, 110

Edwards, D.R. 146
Evans, David J 17

Fellingham, David 14, 44, 160, 178
Fellingham, Louise & Nathan 134
Fellingham, Nathan 15
Forster, Faith 92
Frye, Michael 88

Garrard, Stuart 49
Gauntlett, Henry John 112
Getty, Keith 74
Gibson, John 98
Goodall, Simon 29
Grafstom, Viola 196
Grinnell, Andrew 12

Hadden, David 56, 109
Hare, Susie 24, 35, 40, 65, 97, 115
Haworth, Bryn & Sally 205
Hayward, Rob 72
Hind, David 8, 67
Holden, R. 112
Horley, Doug 73, 79, 104, 203
Howard, Adrian 158
Haworth, Bryn 190
Hughes, Russ 197, 199
Hughes, Tim 100, 108, 131

Iliff, David 110

Jamieson, Kevin 171
Johnston, Philip Lawson 91, 137, 186

Kendrick, Graham 5, 18, 25, 32, 34, 36, 39, 43, 60, 94, 112, 113, 116, 119, 121, 125, 128, 129, 133, 138, 141, 146, 154, 155, 157, 162, 165, 173, 174, 182, 183, 188, 191, 192, 195, 202, 211, 214
Kyle, Paul 99

Leckebusch, Martin E. 35
Lewis, James 106
Lewis, Richard 55, 57, 76, 80, 114, 152, 194, 208
Lomax, Tim 151, 159
Lundy, Damian 181
Lunt, Janet 19

Mark, Robin 86, 130, 164, 180, 226
Markin, Johnny 66
McGregor, Steve 215
Mitchell, Andy 140
Morgan, Patricia 27
Morgan, Trish 225
Morris, David & Liz 163
Morris, David Lyle 92

Oakley, Paul 53, 93, 176, 179, 212
Orange, Chris 123, 127
Owen, Carol 9
Owen, Colin 145

Palmer, David 187
Pantry, John 216
Piercy, Andy 150

Rayner, Andrew 58
Redman, Matt 22, 38, 62, 70, 77, 78, 81, 83, 89, 107, 111, 136, 143, 168, 169, 175, 210
Redman, Matt & Beth 82
Richards, Noel 47, 79, 177, 189, 200, 221
Richards, Noel & Tricia 4, 21, 50, 120, 126, 132, 147, 209
Riley, Ken 51
Roberts, Ian 37
Rogers, Evan 23
Rolinson, Chris 155
Rose, Alan 90
Sandeman, Michael 54
Scott, Kathryn 63
Silvester, Bob 109
Smale, Ian 33, 118
Smith, Martin 30, 65, 75, 77, 117, 122, 135, 149, 167, 169, 170, 201, 204
Sutheran, Jill 20
Sutton, Wes 224

Taylor, Ian 28
Thompson, Steve 60, 165
Thompson, Steve & Velveta 140
Toplady, Augustus Montague 157
Townend, Stuart 6, 41, 42, 61, 74, 124, 139, 171, 198, 213, 219, 223
Turner, Pat 158

Wellington, David 84, 217
White, Ian 161, 185, 218
Wright, James 7, 207, 220, 222

Index of First Lines and Titles

This index gives the first line of each hymn. If a hymn is known by an alternative title, this is also given, but indented and in italics.

A

Abba, Father, let me be	1
All around the world	2
All hail the Lamb	3
All heaven declares	4
All I once held dear	5
All my days	6
All Praise	7
All praise, all honour	7
All the glory	125
Amazing love	8
Amazing love	128
Among the gods	9
An army of ordinary people	10
As sure as gold is precious	11
As we come to your throne	12
At the foot of the cross	13
At your feet we fall	14
Awake, awake O Zion	15

B

Be free	16
Be still, for the presence of the Lord	17
Beautiful Saviour	6
Because of you	179
Be the centre	88
Better is one day	62
Blessed are the humble	18
Breathe	184
Broken for me	19
Broken I stand	20
By your side	21

C

Can a nation be changed?	22
Celebrate	27
Celebrate in the Lord	23
Chosen to go	24
Come and see	25
Come, Lord Jesus	47
Come, now is the time to worship	26
Come on and celebrate	27
Consider it joy	188
Consuming fire	55
Creation is awaiting	28

D

Dancing on holy ground	23
Days of Elijah	180
Deep within my heart	29
Did you feel the mountains tremble?	30
Distant thunder	187

F

Faithful God	31
Falling on my knees	63
Far and near	32
Father God, I wonder	33
Father me	133
Father to you	34
Fire fall	208
For riches of salvation	35
For the cross	82
For this purpose	36
For you have been our hope	37
Friend of sinners	38
From heaven you came	39
From the heights of glory	40
From the squalor of a borrowed stable	41

G

Give thanks	35
Giver of grace	42
God is good	43
God of glory, we exalt your name	44
God of grace	45
Great is the darkness	47
Great is your name	48
Greater grace	46

H

Have you heard the good news?	49
Healing love	161
He has risen	50
He is holy, holy, holy	51
Here I am	52
Here I am	53
Here is the risen Son	54
He rides on the wings of the wind	55
He's given me a garment of praise	56
History maker	75
Holy, holy, holy	51
Holy, holy, so holy	57
Holy mountain	197
Holy Spirit we wait on you	58
Holy Spirit, we welcome you	59
How can I be free from sin?	60
How deep the Father's love for us	61
How good it is	134
How long?	198
How lovely is your dwelling place	62
Hungry, I come to you	63

I

I am a new creation	64
I am learning	65
I believe in angels	66
I believe in the gospel	67
I could sing of your love for ever	149
I could sing unending songs	68
I delight	69
I have heard	70
I kneel down	141
I lift my eyes to the quiet hills	71
I'm accepted, I'm forgiven	72
I'm forever in your love	73
Immanuel	41
In Christ alone	74
Increase in me	140
I really want to worship you, my Lord	221
Is it true today	75
I stand complete in you	45
I surrender	206
I thank you for the precious blood	76
It's all about you	93
It's rising up	77
I've found Jesus	201
I've thrown it all away	78
I want to be out of my depth in your love	79
I will always love your name	53
I will awaken the dawn	80
I will dance, I will sing	81
I will love you for the cross	82
I will offer up my life	83
I will sing of your love	84
I will sing your praises	33
I will testify	85

J

Jesus, all for Jesus	86
Jesus, almighty Saviour	220
Jesus, at your name	87
Jesus be the centre	88
Jesus Christ	89

Jesus, friend for ever	204
Jesus, friend of sinners	176
Jesus is exalted	90
Jesus is our God	91
Jesus is the name we honour	91
Jesus King of the ages	92
Jesus, lover of my soul	93
Jesus put this song into our hearts	94
Jesus shall take the highest honour	95
Jesus, take me as I am	96
Jesus, the Holy One	97
Jesus, we celebrate your victory	98
Jesus, we enthrone you	99
Jesus, you alone	100
Jesus, you are changing me	101
Jesus, you are the Lord of heaven	102

K

Kindle the flame	20
King of kings, majesty	103
King of love	104
Knowing you	5

L

Lamb of God	105
Lead me, Lord	106
Lead me to the cross	60
Let everything that has breath	107
Let God arise	178
Let the Bride say, 'Come'	186
Let the flame burn brighter	202
Light of the World	108
Light of the world	136
Like a child	124
Lion of Judah	226
Living under the shadow of his wings	109
Lord for the years	110
Lord, let your glory fall	111
Lord of glory, we adore you	112
Lord of the years	110
Lord, send the rain	199
Lord, the light of your love	113
Lord, we long to see your glory	114
Lord, what a sacrifice I see	115
Lord, you are so precious to me	116
Lord, you have my heart	117
Lord, you put a tongue in my mouth	118
Lord you've been good to me	119
Love songs from heaven	120

M

Meekness and majesty	121
Men of faith	122
Mercy and love	123
My desire	189
My first love	124
My heart is full	125
My lips shall praise you	126
My Lord, I come to honour you	127
My Lord, what love is this	128
My Redeemer lives	127

N

No scenes of stately majesty	129
Not by might	130
Nothing in this world	131
Nothing shall separate us	132

O

O Father of the fatherless	133
O God of love	134
Oh, lead me	135
O Jesus, Son of God	136
O Lord our God	137
O Lord, your tenderness	138
O my soul, arise and bless your maker	139
Once again	89
One Lord, one faith	140
Only you deserve the glory	48
On the blood-stained ground	141
On the cross	142
O sacred King	143
O taste and see	144
O the blood of my Saviour	145
O, the love of God is boundless	146
Our confidence is in the Lord	147
Our God is great	148
Our God reigns	15
Over the mountains and the sea	149

P

Pour over me	223
Praise God from whom all blessings flow	150
Praise the Lord	151
Prophet, Priest and King	92

R

Rain down	152
Reign in me	153
Rejoice!	154
Restorer of my soul	126
Restore, O Lord	155
Revealer of mysteries	163
Revival	11
River of fire	213
River, wash over me	156
Rock of ages	157

S

Salvation belongs to our God	158
Saviour, I will sing to you	159
Saviour of the world	159
Say it loud	32
Shine, Jesus, shine	113
Shout for joy and sing	160
Shout to the North	122
Sovereign Lord	37
Spirit of the Lord	161
Such love	162
Surely our God	163

T

Take the world but give me Jesus	78
Take us to the river	164
Taste and see	144
Teach me to dance	165
Tell the world	166
Thank you for saving me	167
Thank you for the blood	76
Thank you, thank you for the blood	168
That's why I give my life	222
The beatitudes	18
The cross has said it all	169
The crucible for silver	170
The Father's song	70
The greatest love	115
The happy song	68
The heart of worship	210
The King has come	171
The King of love	171
The latter rain	194
The Lord has led forth	172
The Lord is present here	173
The price is paid	174
There is a louder shout to come	175
There is a voice that must be heard	176
There is power in the name of Jesus	177
There's a pageant of triumph in glory	178
There's a place where the streets shine	179
These are the days	180
The Servant King	39
The Spirit lives to set us free	181
The Spirit of the Lord	182
This Child	183
This is the air I breathe	184
This is the best place	185

This is the mystery	186	We have sung our songs of victory	198	Who paints the skies?	213
This is the time	187			Who sees it all	214
This is your God	121	We humbly pray	199	With all my heart	215
This thankful heart	83	Welcome, King of kings	200	Wonderful grace	216
Though trials will come	188	Well I hear they're singing in the streets	201	*Worshipping the living God*	185
To be in your presence	189	We'll walk the land	202	Worthy	217
To him who loves us	190	We want to see Jesus lifted high	203		
To the King eternal	191	*We will magnify*	137		
To you, O Lord, I lift up my soul	192	*We worship at your feet*	25		
Trust in the Lord	193	What a friend I've found	204		

U

Undignified 81
Upon a cross of shame 207

W

Walk in the light 181
We ask you, O Lord 194
We believe 195
We believe 67
We bow down 196
We have come to a holy mountain 197

What a gift 40
What grace 34
What kind of love is this 205
What love is this? 206
What wondrous love 207
When I pray 208
When I sing my praise 209
When I worship You 209
When the music fades 210
Who can sound the depths of sorrow? 211
Who is there like you? 212

Y

You alone are God 9
You are good to me 42
You are merciful to me 218
You are my anchor 219
You are so good 102
You are the Christ 87
You are the one 29
You are worthy 12
You came from heaven's splendour 220
You laid aside your majesty 221
You laid down your majesty 222
You're the lion of Judah 226
Your love 223
Your mercy flows 224
Your name is great 225